UNITY IN MARRIAGE

UNITY
IN
MARRIAGE

BY

W. J. Fields

Publishing House
St. Louis   London

Concordia Publishing House, Saint Louis 18, Missouri
Concordia Publishing House Ltd., London, W. C. 1
Copyright 1962 by Concordia Publishing House

Third Printing 1974

Library of Congress Catalog Card No. 61-18222
ISBN 0-570-03191-5

To Those
Who Share My Family Unit
JANET
Ann, Lois, Miriam

MANUFACTURED IN THE UNITED STATES OF AMERICA

Foreword

There are three things which should be said by way of introduction to this book. First, it needed to be written. Though there has been much of value written about the Christian interpretation of marriage and family relationships, we have long needed a volume which goes straight to the heart of the essentials of unity in marriage from the Christian point of view. This is a book which Christian people can really use, because it demonstrates clearly the resources which are at their disposal as they work at achieving the unity so important in a marriage.

Second, Pastor Fields should have written this book. He has the theological training, the experience in working with marriages, and the scientific background which are necessary. He is an excellent scholar and a very successful pastor; and he has had the opportunity of working with hundreds of young people as they approach marriage. More important, he understands people, both from the point of view of the cold, hard facts of science and also from the perspective of the Christian way of life. He would be the first to deny that he is so competent; but it is the privilege of the writer of this introduction to state important facts which the author himself would be too modest to include.

Third, this is a sound presentation of the factors essential to a successful marriage relationship, both from the scientific and the Christian point of view. It is possible that some readers from different religious orientations might differ with the author on a few of his illustrations; but these would be on matters of minor significance only. Certainly, the fundamental approach of this book would be acceptable and extremely helpful throughout the whole of Protestantism; and many parts of this book will be welcomed by Christians of other persuasions.

This volume, then, is marked for a highly significant contribution to the Christian approach to marriage. It is deep in meaning; and yet it can be understood by all. It should be read by every clergyman and every Christian couple married or planning to marry. Furthermore, it is valuable reading to anyone doing family-life education or marriage and family counseling.

IOWA STATE UNIVERSITY
Ames, Iowa

DAVID M. FULCOMER, Ph. D.
Professor, Family Sociology,
Marriage Counselor

Preface

Three things spurred the writing of these pages.

While there are many books in the area of family living that are extremely helpful, there are comparatively few that stress as adequately as they should the uniqueness of the Christian home. The Christian family is in many respects no different from any other family, but it does have its own specific Christian philosophy on marriage and a Christian approach to every home problem.

My work as pastor brings me into constant touch with families and their problems. As campus pastor at Iowa State University I have much opportunity to work with people in their early years of marriage and to assist them and counsel them in developing specific Christian approaches to their marriage.

Finally, as over a number of years I have presented material on Christian family living to camps, retreats, workshops, and conferences, I have been asked frequently to make some of the material available in print. Some of this, as it relates specifically to established families, I am attempting to do here.

This book is not in any sense of the word comprehensive, either in the areas that it covers or in the treatment of the areas that it covers. It is not designed to discuss the dating and courtship periods, premarital education and counseling, or specific problem areas in marriage, such as mixed marriage, incompatibility, and unfaithfulness. This little book is meant to lay down the general principles that help guide the Christian's thinking in the matter of marriage, and to help families think through their ideals and goals as Christian families.

This is not a book *about* families. It does not deal with problems facing American families as such. That is the task of the family sociologist. This is rather a book *for* families. It endeavors to point out to the ordinary Christian family that its home is built upon a foundation much deeper than that of the non-Christian home and that this firm foundation makes possible the development of a beautiful and solid superstructure.

It is impossible to give credit for all ideas and concepts that one absorbs over the years. To the many people, both professional and lay, with whom I have worked, to the thousands of students with whom in one way or another I have discussed marriage problems, to the many people at camps and retreats whose discussions always add new insights, and to my own family I offer my profoundest thanks.

I am especially indebted to several people, however. Dr. David Fulcomer, professor of family sociology at Iowa State University in Ames, Iowa, and marriage counselor in the counseling service at Iowa State, as well as specialist consultant to the Committee on Family Life of the National Council of Churches of Christ in America, was especially helpful with his counsel and encouragement. The hours spent in his class as a graduate student, the opportunity later to lead discussions in his classes on various aspects of marriage, and, above all, the rich insights gained from a deep personal friendship with him, have been memorable. He spent many hours in evaluating and in offering concrete suggestions for this manuscript.

Dr. Oscar Feucht, Secretary of Adult Education on the

Board of Parish Education of The Lutheran Church — Missouri Synod, and Secretary of its Family Life Committee, evaluated the manuscript and offered many helpful suggestions. Serving with him on the Family Life Committee of The Lutheran Church — Missouri Synod strengthened my admiration for his frankness, thoroughness, and comprehensive acquaintance with the field of family life.

I am grateful to Jean Kruse and Karl Voelkel, two mature senior students of Iowa State University preparing for their own marriage, who read and discussed the manuscript together and analyzed it from their premarital point of view; also to my secretary, Miss Janice Johnson, who did much of the preliminary typing, and to my wife, who typed the final draft of the manuscript.

In the midst of a secularistic society, Christian homes are influenced inordinately by materialistic values. Strengthening our Christian homes in every way that we can is one of the greatest contributions that we as families can make to our church and society, our nation and our world. May God bless these pages to that end.

W. J. F.

Contents

UNITY IN MARRIAGE

CHAPTER ONE

Working Toward Unity

Each year well over 4,000,000 people vow a lifetime of allegiance to one another in marriage. All of these people have one thing in common — they want to establish happy and harmonious homes. They are certain that, regardless of what problems other marriages might face, theirs is a "perfect" match that will afford a lifetime of marital bliss.

What Happens to Marriages?

Many of these couples come close to this ideal in their marriages. The experiences that they share draw them closely together, and over the years an increasing unity develops between them.

In the early years of their married life many things are new to both of them, and doing them together affords an exciting and unifying adventure. There is the excitement of establishing routines in their marital pattern, the thrill of being close to each other physically, the delights they find in discovering and sharing each other's likes and hobbies. These are the exhilarating experiences which most young married couples enjoy.

As their marriage matures, their unity is solidified and

deepened more by the things that they *feel* together than by the things that they *do* together, in the problems that they face and overcome, the budgetary difficulties that they solve, the sickness they endure, the burdens they carry, the sorrows they share, the successes they enjoy, the failures they master, the concerns for and responsibility toward their children that they undergo — in all of this they find themselves drawn to each other and comfortably dependent upon each other. One experience after another knits them together a little more firmly than they were before. They realize an increasing oneness and togetherness that makes their living together something that belongs to both of them. They feel like one married woman, to whom a new bride was rejoicing about her marital bliss and who replied: "If you think that it's wonderful now, wait until you are married a few years. It gets more wonderful all the time."

For too many of these couples something altogether different happens. They never achieve the family solidarity for which they so much hope on their wedding day. They never succeed in meshing their personalities. As far as growing together is concerned, their marriage never gets out of low gear. They never fully and profoundly know and understand each other. They misjudge and often impugn each other's motives. They manifest a growing resentment and bitterness toward each other. Their experiences in living together pull them apart rather than draw them together. And finally they admit their failure to make satisfactory adjustments, and legalize that failure by procuring a divorce, probably on the grounds of "incompatibility" or "mental cruelty."

Still others of these couples live together for a lifetime in what appears to everyone — except perhaps those who know them most intimately — as a satisfactory marriage. They establish themselves in their community and church; they rear a family; they achieve financial status. They give every external impression of being solid citizens with happy and well-adjusted home lives. Others might even think of them as being "ideally suited to each other." But they never achieve in their marriage what they want to achieve and what they ought to achieve. They never attain a genuine, relaxed, and completely satisfying happiness in and with each other. They never develop the security of being comfortably complete in each other. They display little mutual understanding, helpfulness, loyalty, and encouragement to each other. Despite superficial appearances their marriage is one in name only. Where it really matters, in the deeper and more profound aspects of their interpersonal living, they fail. For all practical purposes they are separated from each other — they are "miles apart" — though they live together under the same roof and spend many hours together. Although legally they are united with each other in marriage, spiritually and emotionally they are far from being united with each other in an enduring relationship of love.

MARRIAGE CONSISTS OF PEOPLE

The degree of happiness or unhappiness that the marriage affords depends entirely upon the persons involved. Marriage becomes precisely what the people who constitute the marriage make it. There is nothing intrinsic in the state of marriage itself that guarantees happiness or that spells unhappiness. Strictly speaking, marriages never succeed and marriages never fail. It is the *people* in marriage who either succeed or fail in their relationships with each other. If a marriage is happy, it is because the people involved have made it a happy one. If a marriage is unhappy, it is because the people involved have made it unhappy.

No two people are ever so perfectly and ideally matched for each other that their very meeting assures them automatically a lifetime of happiness together. Whenever a person sees a happy and successful marriage, he can be sure that he is seeing two people who have worked consciously and conscientiously at making the marriage succeed; two people who, as mature adults, have devoted many hours to working out their problems, their differences, their likes and dislikes; two people who in the crucible of their everyday experiences have learned the meaning of understanding and compromise and love. Successful marriages demand time and energy and intelligent effort on the part of each person involved in the relationship.

Marriage Demands Many Personal Adjustments

In marriage two individuals are brought together who vary from each other in many respects. Each is of a different sex, and each has different psychological needs, both as a person and as a representative of his sex. Each comes from a different home background. Each has had a different set of experiences, and each has, because of his background, learned to react in a different manner to the same experiences. What may be repulsive to one may be accepted by the other. One word, or one experience, may conjure up in the mind of one a whole panorama of traumatic experiences, whereas it may result in a pleasant reaction for the other. Each of the persons has his own particular frustrations and fears, hopes and dreams. In addition, each has his own expectations of what he hopes to contribute to the marriage and what he expects to derive from it.

Now these two people "come to be united." They propose to weld their lives together. From henceforth they will no longer live two separate and independent lives, but one life, a life together — a shared life. The experiences of each are to become part of the experiences of the other. This blending and unifying process is not an automatic result of the repetition of the marriage vow. It involves a lifelong process of unselfish and complete dedication of the one to the other and to the building of their lives together.

In this process innumerable problems need attention and adjustment. To the degree that they are met constructively and solved adequately a happy marriage results. But their solution is always a distinctly individual solution between the two persons involved. Since each of them is a unique individual, different from every other individual in the world, and since the two of them together are a unique couple, different from every other couple in the world, it is impossible to establish a panacea that automatically applies to all couples and provides for them an infallible guide. What procedures work for one couple under one combination of circumstances and personalities may not work at all for another couple with their particular circumstances and personalities. Each couple must achieve its own unity and establish its own family pattern according to its individual needs and circumstances. What may seem like a most unideal solution to other people might be the very circumstances under which a given family is meeting and fulfilling the needs of each of its members and deriving the most happiness.

By way of illustration, one of the essential areas where a high degree of unity must be developed is in the matter of finances. *How* this matter is resolved is less important than *that* it is resolved. In one family the husband may be in complete charge of the financial aspects of the home, and the wife knows little about the bills, the securities, and the general expenses. In another home the husband may turn his pay check over to his wife as soon as he receives it, and she manages the household budget from then on. Another family may set up a system of allowances, where both husband and wife have a certain sum of money monthly or weekly for which neither is accountable to the other. They may have separate bank accounts or joint bank accounts. They may do their shopping together or they may do it separately. In one family I know the wife satisfies her need for some money of her own, to do with as she pleases, by receiving from her golf-loving husband dollar for dollar all that he spends for golf. She thus has at her disposal an extra-budgetary sum of money which she can feel free to spend as she sees fit. Whatever the solution, the important thing is that it be mutually satisfactory to those who work it out.

Each Family Is Unique

This principle holds true for every aspect of marriage. Each family is facing its own peculiar set of circumstances and must in its own way, within the frame of reference of the personalities involved, meet and adjust to its own situation. Here, for example, is a workingman whose occupation keeps him on the job eight hours a day, from eight to five. The adjustments of his family will be altogether different from those of the family in which the husband works from midnight to eight A. M. Then there is the man whose vocation is one of the professions. He knows no eight-hour day, but is on constant call. Family plans may often be upset at a moment's notice. The telephone may buzz with business calls at all hours. The pattern that the family develops must adjust to this "schedule." Here is a salesman. His work takes him away from home for long stretches at a time. He may get home weekends, but at other times he is not an immediate part of his family circle. His role in the family is different from that of the husband and father who can spend the majority of his nonworking hours with those whom he loves.

It is impossible, therefore, and unfair, for one family to compare itself with another. Members of one family might long for some of the circumstances under which other families live. That is only natural. In their own situation people are constantly face to face with their own problem areas, and often they see only the desirable factors of another set of circumstances. Thus they are prone to compare the undesirable factors of their own marriage situation with what looks to them like the desirable factors of another marriage situation. They may forget that their marriage situation, which has some undesirable factors involved in it, has also many desirable factors, and that another marriage situation that seems to have so many desirable factors also has many undesirable factors of its own. While they are comparing their undesirable factors with the desirable ones in another family, that other family may be comparing its own undesirable factors with the desirable ones in theirs.

To wish to have what the Joneses have, to dream of being able to do what the Joneses do, to pray that one's spouse would be more like Mr. or Mrs. Jones, may be delightful daydreaming, but it is completely unrealistic. The fact of the matter is that one's spouse is what he is, and the circumstances under which one lives are what they are. Sometimes the spouses or the circumstances might be altered somewhat to make them more desirable, but one of the marks of maturity is to be able to accept gracefully, to adjust cheerfully, and to find happiness readily within the framework of circumstances that exist. Mature people have learned to accept people and circumstances as they are. They have "learned in whatsoever state they are, therewith to be content." (Philippians 4:11)

What Constitutes Happiness in Marriage?

People frequently make the mistake of assuming that happiness depends upon external factors. They link their happiness with materialistic concerns — a fine home, a good income, a comfortable security, health, reputation — and they assume that the person whose material concerns are all provided for should be among the happiest people in the world. I don't know how many times I have heard it said about a woman that she should be most happy indeed because she has a fine home with all the conveniences and all of the financial security she could possibly want. The assumption is that because she has "things" she should therefore automatically have happiness. This is the error that concludes that if a family moves from a $10,000 home to a $30,000 home, or if a family's income increases from $300 a month to $900 a month, that its happiness should therefore treble.

A successful businessman friend of mine was hospitalized with ulcers. When told of his illness, an acquaintance remarked, "What does he have to worry about? Look at how successful his business is." It certainly is true that external factors and materialistic considerations can contribute to one's happiness and contentment. Solomon understood that a lack of sufficient material blessings as well as an abundance of them could cause many problems. So he prayed, "Give me neither poverty nor riches; feed me with food convenient for me, lest I be full and deny Thee and say, Who is the Lord? or lest I be poor and steal and take the name of my God in vain." (Proverbs 30:8, 9)

External factors in themselves are not the foundation of one's happiness. In the final analysis happiness never originates from anything outside ourselves; it originates from within ourselves. Some people are happy with little; others are not happy even with much. It all depends upon the people. I have known people who are extremely poor, with very few of the comforts and conveniences that go to make up twentieth-century living, who are among the most contented people in the world. And I have known people with much in terms of material possessions who never knew the meaning of contentment and happiness. They never found it because they kept looking in the wrong places.

Iowa State University has a housing project for its married students. Most of the one thousand units are barracks. Families are crowded. There is no central heating. There is little play area for children and even less grass. Financial situations are pinched, sometimes desperate. Sometimes wives as well as husbands must work in order to be able to stay in school. But visiting in this area is a joy. One senses immediately an understanding of the basic values of life. There is a family solidarity among most of these couples that is a delight to behold. They are working together for a common goal. They are willing to sacrifice and to laugh at the amount of "hamburger" they consume and the many inexpensive recipes that they have learned. Neighbors help one another. Paying for baby-sitting is unheard of. People do this for one another. If a mother in one unit has a baby, the other families on the row take care of the husband for meals during the hospitalization. Couples can afford few nights out, but they have learned to enjoy the inexpensive pleasures. They get together to play bridge; they appreciate the fellowship of one another over a cup of coffee; they come in a group to

the church student center to challenge each other in ping-
pong. Again and again these couples have told me after they
had graduated and established themselves, that although they
enjoyed more comfortable circumstances financially and materially, they never again experienced the togetherness that
Pammel Court, their married housing unit, afforded them.

They who have learned to find happiness wherever they
are and to be content with whatever they have, have learned
one of the secrets of happiness. "Happiness is where you
find it." It is always a matter, not of material circumstances,
but of one's reaction to those circumstances. Those people
are truly happy who have learned to find it in themselves and
in the circumstances in which they live.

Christ left us a classic on what constitutes true happiness.
In the Beatitudes from His Sermon on the Mount He lists
some characteristics which incidentally stop us short because
they are different from what we sometimes conceive of as
the basis for happiness:

> How happy are the humble-minded, for the kingdom of
> heaven is theirs!
> How happy are those who know what sorrow means, for
> they will be given courage and comfort!
> Happy are those who claim nothing, for the whole earth
> will belong to them!
> Happy are those who are hungry and thirsty for goodness,
> for they will be fully satisfied!
> Happy are the merciful, for they will have mercy shown
> to them!
> Happy are the utterly sincere, for they will see God!
> Happy are those who make peace, for they will be known
> as sons of God!
> Happy are those who have suffered persecution for the
> cause of goodness, for the kingdom of heaven is theirs!
> And what happiness will be yours when people blame you

and ill-treat you and say all kinds of slanderous things against you for My sake! Be glad then, yes, be tremendously glad — for your reward in heaven is magnificent. They persecuted the prophets before your time in exactly the same way.[1]

In his book *Your God Is Too Small* Phillips says of these Beatitudes that Christ "gave a complete reversal of conventional values and ambitions, though many people miss this undoubted fact because of the poetic form and archaic language. . . . Their revolutionary character becomes apparent at once, however, if we substitute the word 'happy' for the word 'blessed.' "[2] Phillips then goes on to contrast the normal concepts that people have had through the centuries, comparing them with what he interprets Jesus to mean:

Most people think:

Happy are the pushers: for they get on in the world.

Happy are the hard-boiled: for they never let life hurt them.

Happy are they who complain: for they get their own way in the end.

Happy are the blasé: for they never worry over their sins.

Happy are the slave-drivers: for they get results.

Happy are the knowledgeable men of the world: for they know their way around.

Happy are the troublemakers: for people have to take notice of them.

Jesus Christ said:

Happy are those who realize their spiritual poverty: they have already entered the kingdom of Reality.

Happy are they who bear their share of the world's pain:

[1] Matthew 5:3-12, from J. B. Phillips, *The New Testament in Modern English* (New York: The Macmillan Company, 1959).

[2] J. B. Phillips, *Your God Is Too Small,* (New York: The Macmillan Company), p. 101.

in the long run they will know more happiness than those who avoid it.

Happy are they who accept life and their own limitations: they will find more in life than anybody.

Happy are those who long to be truly "good": they will fully realize their ambition.

Happy are those who are ready to make allowances and to forgive: they will know the love of God.

Happy are those who are real in their thoughts and feelings: in the end they will see the ultimate Reality, God.

Happy are those who help others to live together: they will be known to be doing God's work.[3]

CHAPTER TWO

Unifying Factors in a Christian Home

The thesis of this book is that Christian homes have in their essence ingredients that non-Christian homes do not have.

It is true, of course, that non-Christian homes can be, and oftentimes are, happy homes. Many people who have no religious conviction whatever succeed in building solid marriages. They are mature and thoughtful individuals, make adjustments well, and adapt themselves to each other. Even people whose moral standards and ethical ideals are on a low level may establish happy homes, because they find a togetherness in what they consider important and worth striving for. Their standards and their philosophies may be detrimental to society, but they are bound together by the common goals that they share. It should be said, too, that mixed marriages, either in religion or race or age, may develop into happy ones.

[3] J. B. Phillips, pp. 101, 102.

The percentage of happy homes is statistically lower among mixed marriages, but percentages do not always apply to individual instances. Any one specific mixed marriage may be composed of people who possess the extraordinary maturity that is needed to overcome the additional difficulties and to make the additional adjustments.

CHRISTIAN HOMES SHOULD BE THE HAPPIEST HOMES

It is true, though, that whereas nonreligious, and specifically non-Christian, homes may be happy ones, Christian homes ought to be happier. With their particular ideals and motivations and philosophies Christians have something to bring to their marriage, and a foundation on which to build it, that non-Christians do not have. The home that is built by two genuine and sincere Christians (not merely nominal church members) has a "plus" factor that helps it achieve what other homes, happy though they may be, cannot fully achieve.

WHEN IS A HOME CHRISTIAN?

In his book *Helping Families Through the Church* Oscar Feucht lists and describes seven characteristics of a genuinely Christian home. By his standards, a Christian home is much more than one in which the family has a church membership and in which there are family prayers and Bible reading habits. It reaches out beyond that. Feucht lists:

1. A Common Faith in Christ as the Savior. Both husband and wife have understood the tremendousness of the redemption of Christ in their lives and have committed themselves to living for that Christ. They have become "new creatures" in Christ. They have become "Christ-men" and "Christ-women," people "in whom Christ has come to live, not for a moment, not for a day, but always." This personal, sincere, and individual commitment to Christ by all members of the family is the first ingredient of a Christian home.

2. A Christian Concept of Marriage. Christians hold marriage sacred and inviolate. The three principles that characterize their view of marriage are: (a) that it is monogamous; (b) that it demands fidelity on the part of both husband and wife; (c) that it is for life.

3. A Christian Attitude Toward Parenthood. Christian parents welcome children as blessings of God. In parenthood they come to a point of fulfillment. They regard parenthood as their highest vocation.

4. Christian Teaching and Guidance. Christian homes teach six essentials of the Christian faith and life: (a) a sense of security through the love and care of God; (b) moral values — a proper sense of right and wrong; (c) a solid foundation on which to build life: a thorough understanding of the Word of God; (d) skills of worship: prayer, Bible reading and study, the art of living by the Word of God; (e) the way of forgiveness in Christ; (f) relationship to the holy Christian church, the body of Christ.

5. Christian Harmony and Right Relationships Between the Members of the Family. Christian love reigns supreme. There is respect for all the individuals in the family, good cheer and a radiant spirit, temperament control, emotional maturity.

6. Accepting God's Values and God's Will. It uses God's "scale of values" — not that of society — "in putting a price tag on all things."

7. A Christian Atmosphere. "A strongly Christian home has a spirit about it that is soon noticeable. It is more than 'religious.' It is deeper than routine talk of 'the church' and congregational affairs. It reflects the presence of Jesus Christ in the hearts of the members of the family." [1]

ATTITUDES AND CONCEPTS

In their book *Building a Successful Marriage* Landis and Landis say:

The future of any marriage will be affected by such factors as the personality traits of the husband and wife, their family

[1] Oscar Feucht, *Helping Families Through the Church* (St. Louis: Concordia Publishing House, 1971), pp. 10—22.

backgrounds, and some of the attitudes they hold. In truth, *their attitudes will have far more to do with their success in marriage* than will the intensity of the love they feel for each other on their wedding day. *Their marriage will be affected in great measure by their concept of what marriage is,* their ideas of what it will require of them, and what they hope to receive from it.[2] (Italics mine)

Attitudes and Marriage Happiness

The Christian religion has much to say about "attitudes." In fact, the entire Christian ethic is directed to the inner attitudes rather than to the outward actions of people. Jesus was always more concerned with the motive of people's behavior than with the behavior itself. He was never contented with the external righteousness of the scribes and Pharisees of His day. Outwardly they kept all the rules, but Jesus always looked at the motivation for keeping the rules. As it is wrong to do what is wrong, so it may also be wrong to do what is right. As T. S. Eliot put it: "The greatest treason [is] to do the right deed for the wrong reason." [3]

The central motivation for all Christian living is love. The Christian has learned to know and to understand the love of God for him. He has become the recipient of that love in Jesus Christ. And because of Christ he has now been remade. The love of Christ for him evokes a love for Christ in him. He has understood the revolutionary fact that God loves all men, saints and sinners alike, and his commitment to Christ causes him to respond with the same kind of love for all men. "We love because He first loved us" (1 John 4:19 RSV). He first of all "loves the Lord, his God, with all

[2] Judson T. Landis and Mary G. Landis, *Building a Successful Marriage,* 3d ed. (Englewood Cliffs, N. J.: Prentice-Hall, Inc., 1958), p. 3.

[3] T. S. Eliot, *Murder in the Cathedral* (New York: Harcourt, Brace and Company, 1935), p. 44.

his heart and with all his soul and with all his mind" (Matthew 22:37). This is the first commandment. This is the power of his life. And because of this love for God he is also able then to "love his neighbor as himself" (Matthew 22:39). Sin to the Christian is much more than merely breaking a few rules or social customs; sin is a lack of love. Pride, selfishness, envy, quarreling, bickering — one could go down the entire catalog, and at the base of them all is lovelessness. And on the other hand, morality and ethics involves a great deal more than merely abiding by a list of superficial rules and refraining from some gross sins. It is always based on love, love for God and love for one's fellowman. No matter how rigidly one might live an exemplary life, if the behavior is motivated by anything else than love, it is not Christian.

The Meaning of Love

There is perhaps no place where the English language expresses its poverty more than in its use of the word "love." The word is used to express all different kinds of emotions and reactions. We say, "I love my parents; I love my brothers and sisters; I love my friends; I love shrimp; I love history; I love the color blue; I love my work; I love my wife; I love my children; I love my home." In each of these instances the word describes an altogether different emotion. Yet we use the same word to express them all.

The Greeks did a little better. They had three different words with three different connotations, all of which are translated simply "love" in English: *eros, philia,* and *agape.*

Eros

Eros is what we might call the "getting" love. It is the feeling we get when something pleases us and satisfies our needs. "I love food; I love to bowl." In a sense our romantic love is included in the concept *eros*. "I love this man or woman because he or she pleases me." "It is such a wonderful feeling to know that you are loved." *Eros* is the feeling of desire — not necessarily sexual, although it may be. There is nothing wrong with the *eros*-type love, but spiritually, from the Christian point of view, it is the lowest kind of love.

Philia

Philia is the "sharing" kind of love. This is the kind of love that exists between friends. Certainly it exists also between spouses. We love to be with each other because we benefit mutually from our association. We are good for each other. We have interests and hobbies and needs and problems to share. We give and we take. We understand each other.

Agape

Agape reaches out beyond both of these. It is the word that the Scripture uses to define God: "God is Love" (1 John 4:8), and it is the kind of love that marks the Christian life. It is never concerned with what it can get, but only with what it can give. It loves for the sake of loving. It keeps on loving even when there is no love in return, even when it is impossible to like. It is determined not by whether the recipient is worthy of the love, but exists for its own sake. It is this *agape* that is described in the great chapter on Christian love in the New Testament, 1 Corinthians 13. This *agape* is defined for us in Scripture: "Herein is love, not that we love God, but that He loved us and sent His Son to be the Propitiation for our sins" (1 John 4:10). Or again: "Hereby perceive we the love of God, because He laid down His life for us"

(1 John 3:16). Or: "God commendeth His love toward us in that, while we were yet sinners, Christ died for us" (Romans 5:8). Christ died for us just because we were so helpless and so separated from Him.

Of this *agape* William Cole says: "Love is *not*, in Biblical terms, an emotion. It is an orientation, an attitude, of the total personality, 'heart and soul and mind and strength.' It is an outgoing concern for what is loved that seeks to serve and to give."[4]

All Three in the Home

All three of these kinds of love show themselves in the Christian home. In many homes love never gets beyond the *eros* stage. In some, indeed, the chief attraction is sexual, and when in the passing years the "erotic" appeal of the other wears off, there is nothing left. Many times the "loves" of spouses remain shallow and selfish. Each displays his love for the other as long as the other is lovable. When the spouse acts and reacts in a manner that is not lovable and pleasing, then the other's love grows cold. Each begins to think of marriage in terms of "his rights," and arguments ensue.

In other homes love develops to the *philia* level. The couple achieves a measure of adjustment. They find happiness and enjoyment in each other. They have many things in common, and their marriage is successful because they have been "well matched." This is important and it makes for happiness in marriage. Marriages in which love has gone beyond the *eros* stage to the *philia* stage are beginning to find a measure of happiness.

In the Christian home, however, love is to get beyond

[4] William Graham Cole, *Sex in Christianity and Psychoanalysis* (New York: Oxford University Press, 1955), p. 24.

both of these kinds of love to the highest level. The spouses have for each other not only a romantic love, not only a sharing love, but permeating both, also a Christian love, *agape*. They love each other simply for the sake of loving. They love because they are persons who have been touched with the love of God, and they do not know how to do anything else but love, even when the spouse seems unlovable. This *agape* is the "plus" factor in Christian homes.

Landis and Landis say that "attitudes" are a most important factor in home happiness. The Christian religion has much to say about attitudes.

CHRISTIAN "CONCEPTS" OF MARRIAGE

Landis and Landis say also that the "concept of what marriage is" is of fundamental importance to a couple's success. The Christian religion also has a specific "concept of what marriage is." It is some of these concepts that are requisites for the happiest marriage.

Marriage Is Permanent

1. In the Christian home it is assumed, without reservation or question of any kind, that marriage is a permanent estate established by God. For the Christian, marriage is much more than merely a sociological development to meet the demands of the society in which we live; it is rather an inviolable ordinance of God, permanent and lifelong in endurance. It is much more than a contract into which one enters, even though it is sometimes called a "marriage contract";[5] it is a lifelong commitment that carries with it moral overtones. Unlike many contracts it has no escape clause.

---

[5] Elton and Pauline Trueblood, *The Recovery of Family Life* (New York: Harper and Brothers, 1953), pp. 43—46, present an excellent development of this point.

It is not an agreement that may be broken simply by mutual consent. It is the unbreakable pledge "not to part from thee till death us do part," "for richer or for poorer, for better or for worse, in sickness and in health."

This attitude toward the permanence of marriage is basic. Under no circumstances does a Christian call this principle into question. He has no reservation of any kind that his union might be a trial marriage and that, if it doesn't "work out," he can always call a halt to it. He thinks of monogamy and lifelong faithfulness to his spouse not merely as a pattern that is followed by respectable people, but as a standard established by God Himself, and to which he is unalterably committed. Marriage to him is "the free acceptance of a bond." [6] He is not thereby "made blind to the physical attractiveness of women other than his wife, but the possibility of making love to them is ruled out in advance. One big decision makes a host of minor decisions unnecessary. Free love, like private marriage, is a contradiction in terms, for conjugal love in many directions is real love in none." [7]

The Christian's motivation for this pattern of thought is not coercion nor the force of public opinion; it is rather that God's way has become his way. Having become "a new creature in Christ" (2 Corinthians 5:17; Galatians 6:15), he has submitted his will completely to that of Christ. He knows that marriage is a part of God's order of creation (Genesis 2:18 ff.; Matthew 19:4 ff.), and the permanency of this institution is something he takes for granted.

With this kind of attitude the couple has a basic framework upon which to do their marital building. Whenever adjustment and personality problems arise, as they do in

[6] Trueblood, p. 48.

[7] Trueblood, p. 49.

every home, their first thought is not one of leaving the spouse because their marriage is "on the rocks." Their basic thought pattern rather goes something like this: "We are married. We promised ourselves to each other for a lifetime. Marriage is for 'keeps,' and we are in this thing together for a long time. Therefore we should not only make satisfactory adjustments to each other, but we should begin to build together to make the welfare and happiness of our union one of mutual concern."

This set of mind makes all the difference in the world. If there is even the slightest feeling on the part of one or the other partner that marriage is anything less than permanent, then that spouse is in no position to give his total unqualified self to the other, and he certainly is not in a position to work wholeheartedly and completely in making his marriage succeed.

It is necessary, too, that *both* partners approach their marriage with the same attitude if they are to achieve the happiest kind of adjustment. Marriage demands all of the cooperative efforts of both partners without reservation or qualification. If either has a psychological barrier to a full and complete commitment, he will be contributing to the undermining of the family relationships. In a Christian home both partners begin with the same attitude toward the permanence of marriage.

Christian Personalities at Work

2. In a Christian home the individual partners are Christian, not in name only, but in fact. The characteristics that make for a good Christian also make for a good spouse. The traits of a genuine Christian personality, like understanding and patience, love and kindness, helpfulness and loyalty, faithfulness and selflessness, are characteristics which every

Christian, married or unmarried, is constantly striving to develop. As one who is dedicated to walking Christ's way he is always striving to become more the kind of person that Christ wants him to be. He wants to "grow in grace" (2 Peter 3:18). He wants to "bring into captivity every thought to the obedience of Christ" (2 Corinthians 10:5). Each day he wants to put his Christian principles into practice a little more consistently. He is constantly working at this; he is constantly praying for this.

Now when two such Christians with these same goals come to the marriage estate, each of them begins to lose himself in the service and interests of the other. Each can no longer be concerned primarily with his own happiness, his own interests, his own rights. Each, because of his concept of Christian love, and by virtue of a personality built upon that precept of outgoing love, becomes totally absorbed in the rights and happiness of the other. Each lives for what St. Francis of Assisi prayed, that he seek not so much "to be consoled as to console; not to be understood, but to understand; not to be loved, but to love." He understands, as St. Francis also continues, that "it is in giving that we receive, in forgetting that we find ourselves, in pardoning that we are pardoned." The complete prayer ascribed to Francis of Assisi is well known:

> O Lord, make me an instrument of Thy peace.
> Where there is hatred, let me sow love;
> Where there is injury, pardon;
> Where there is discord, union;
> Where there is doubt, faith;
> Where there is despair, hope;
> Where there is darkness, light;
> Where there is sadness, joy;
> O Lord, grant that we seek
>   not to be consoled, but to console;
>   not to be understood, but to understand;
>   not to be loved, but to love.

For it is in giving that we receive,
in forgetting that we find ourselves,
in pardoning that we are pardoned,
and in dying that we are born to eternal life. Amen.

The Christian understands, too, that his Christian virtues never exist in a vacuum. They always manifest themselves to people. The fact that one is a Christian makes a difference in the way he conducts his business or operates his farm or drives his truck or washes his dishes. It makes a difference, too, in the way he conducts himself at home. As a Christian he is "the light of the world" (Matthew 5:14). A part of the world for which he is to be a light is his home. He understands well the adage that "charity (love) begins at home," and he knows, too, that the light that shines farthest must always shine brightest right at home. Hence he is constantly trying to live as a Christian in his home, striving to display there toward those whom he loves all the consideration and self-control and patience that he does toward the boss at work, the secretary in the office, the neighbor next door who drops by to unload her problems.

Christians Believe in the Reality of Sin

3. The Christian furthermore begins with a specific philosophy toward life. He believes in the reality of sin. To him sin is not merely a generic term, a vague generality. It is something real and practical and individual.

He believes also in the universality of sin. He knows therefore, not just academically, but in fact, that there is no perfect person on earth, not even his spouse. He knows, too, that sin will always manifest itself. It is not simply a theological concept; it is a practical reality. It shows itself not only in the form of crass evils of society, like murder, drunkenness, adultery, stealing, and the like, but also in what we call human weakness and imperfection, in disloyalties and temper tantrums, in selfishness and thoughtlessness, in lack of self-control and self-discipline. St. Paul concludes his dissertation on this matter by saying, "I find, then, a law that, when I would do good, evil is present with me." (Romans 7:21)

Knowing this, the Christian does not expect to find perfection where it is impossible to find it. He expects his spouse to react like the sinful human being that she is. He certainly is not surprised when he sees her imperfections manifest themselves. So when his wife is in a disagreeable mood, when she loses her patience, when she gives evidence of selfishness or envy, this does not "throw him." He knows that he is seeing the manifestation of sin in her behavior. When the husband appears thoughtless or inconsiderate, unappreciative or uncommunicative, the wife is not "thrown" into a state of unhappiness, because she believes in the fact of sin and knows that her husband, too, is a sinner.

It is one of the strange phenomena of so much of home life that Christians are quick to say that they believe that no one is perfect and yet they become so completely impatient when they see that imperfection in action in their homes. Christians are not surprised at anything that they find in their spouses. They know that sin is real.

Christians Understand Forgiveness

4. The Christian not only accepts and understands the reality of sin. He knows, too, the meaning of forgiveness. He has experienced it in his life over and over again. The basis of his relationship with God is his own forgiveness in Christ. And his willingness to forgive in turn now marks his relationship with others. Day after day he forgives and forgets, as Christ has forgiven him. He lives by the principle,

"Be ye kind one to another, tenderhearted, forgiving one another, even as God for Christ's sake hath forgiven you" (Ephesians 4:32). Each day he clears out of his system all peeves and grudges. He never "lets the sun go down on his wrath" (Ephesians 4:26). He does not allow grievances and hurts to mount to bitterness and hate. Forgiveness flows readily from his heart, so that his closet is always completely empty of all skeletons.

But not only does he forgive and forget, fully and completely; he also is ready always to seek the forgiveness of the one he loves. He understands that when he prays, "Forgive us our trespasses as we forgive those who trespass against us" (Matthew 6:12), he is not only seeking the pardon of a forgiving God, but he is also obligating himself to be a pardoning and *pardon-seeking* person. It is easy in a general way to mouth our requests for divine forgiveness and to say to God, as we do in the fifth petition of the Lord's Prayer, "I am sorry." But it is much more difficult, and it takes a great deal more humility and swallowing of pride, to see our individual sins for what they are, to stop all rationalizing them away, and to stand before the one we have offended and to say to him, "I am sorry. I have sinned against you. Please forgive me." But the genuine Christian will do that. It is a part of the way he thinks and lives.

The Holy Triangle

5. Another feature of the Christian home is this, that the husband and the wife are not first of all dedicated to each other. We usually assume that for a happy home it is necessary that they be. In a genuinely Christian home, however, there is always a triangle — a holy triangle. Both husband and wife are dedicated first of all to a "third party" —

to Christ. This love to Christ makes their relationship to each other not less meaningful, but more. As each gives his life in commitment to Christ and totally dedicates himself to living for that Christ, his relationship to his spouse is also enriched. This triangle becomes the cementing factor between husband and wife. They are building their life now on a common foundation. Each has found a wholeness and completeness in Christ, and he shares that wholeness, that completeness with his spouse. Christian homes welcome and keep this "Third Party" in their midst. For them the prayer "Come, Lord Jesus, be our Guest" does not say nearly enough. Christ is vastly more than a "guest." He is part of the family.

"The relation of the husband and wife and children is to be 'in the Lord' (Colossians 3:18, 20). Christians are admonished to 'take a wife in sanctification and honor' (1 Thessalonians 4:3-7). Christian widows, if they marry, are to marry 'in the Lord' " (1 Corinthians 7:39).[8] A Christian home without Christ at the center is a contradiction and an impossibility. Christian homes are composed of Christian people, and Christian people are people who love Christ and serve Christ and

[8] Statement on Interfaith Marriages, *Proceedings* of the Forty-fourth Regular Convention of The Lutheran Church — Missouri Synod, San Francisco, Calif., 1959, p. 211.

The passages mentioned in the quotation are Colossians 3:18, 20 RSV: "Wives, be subject to your husbands, as is fitting in the Lord. . . . Children, obey your parents in everything, for this pleases the Lord."

1 Thessalonians 4:3-7 RSV: "For this is the will of God, your sanctification: that you abstain from immorality; that each one of you know how to take a wife for himself in holiness and honor, not in the passion of lust like heathen who do not know God; that no man transgress and wrong his brother in this matter, because the Lord is an avenger in all these things, as we solemnly forewarned you. For God has not called us for uncleanness, but in holiness."

1 Corinthians 7:39 RSV: "A wife is bound to her husband as long as he lives. If the husband dies, she is free to be married to whom she wishes, only in the Lord."

are committed to Christ. They are "in Christ" (2 Corinthians 5:17). Just as a person "in" business or "in" law or "in" agriculture devotes himself to that pursuit, so a person who is "in" Christ devotes himself to following Christ. He is a "new creature." Whatever he does — also establishing a home — he does "in" Christ.

God Is Involved in Marriage

6. Finally, the Christian attitude toward the home recognizes that marriage has implications far beyond its own walls. The Christian never says, "What we do is our business. If our marriage fails, no one but us is hurt." He understands very well that marriage is not a private affair, but that it has social implications and involves the concerns and happiness of many people. He knows that marriage is the God-ordained foundation of society. Upon it rests the structure of our entire civilization. Whether or not a home life is happy affects not only the spouses involved, but their *children,* their *parents,* their *relatives,* and their *friends* as well. Moreover, the *church* is affected, because what happens to any given home happens to a part of the community of saints at that place. The entire *community* is affected, because the stability of the community depends upon the stability of its families. As a chain is no stronger than its weakest link, so no community is stronger than the families of which it is constituted. The entire *nation* is involved. History shows that the decline of many great world powers occurred in direct proportion to the weakening of that nation's home ties. When marriage and the home were no longer considered sacred, then the floodgates were opened for destructive moral and ethical standards to prevail, thus weakening the character and integrity of the nation.

But most important of all, *God* has a stake in the family.

Marriage is His institution. He ordained it that two people might complement each other and perpetuate the race He had established. God made men and women, not merely that there might be variety in the human species, but that they might belong together, that they might complete one another, that they might live for one another, that they might "subdue His creation" together (Genesis 1:28). Any taking lightly of this estate is a direct slap in the face to God, who conceived and established this way of living together in the first place. Marriage, the Christian understands, is sacred, to be unmarred by any human intervention.

The Christian home should be the strongest, the most ideal, the happiest kind of home. If it is not, the trouble lies not with Christianity, but with Christians. The Christian religion provides the ingredients, the philosophy, the principles, and the motivation that make for solid, happy home life. If Christians do not achieve this goal, the cause for the failure lies not in the principles, but in the Christians' inconsistency in carrying out those principles, or worse yet, in completely ignoring them. Christians have, by everything that they hold dear, not only all the characteristics that ordinarily bring people into and keep them together in family units; they have also the potential of a home life that is more close-knit and love-motivated than any other home on earth.

CHAPTER THREE

The Unity of Love

The Christian's life is one of constant moral struggle. He knows what he ought to become, but he is always falling short of his goal. He is constantly undergoing the struggle that St. Paul knew: "The good that I would I do not, but the evil which I would not, that I do" (Romans 7:19). He understands very well that he has "not already attained" (Philippians 3:12), but he is constantly "reaching forth unto those things which are before," and pressing "toward the mark for the prize of the high calling of God in Jesus Christ" (Philippians 3:13, 14). He is always striving, to the very day of his death, to "grow up into Him in all things, which is the Head, even Christ" (Ephesians 4:15), always reaching out for moral perfection, always striving to achieve his ideals. He never reaches them, but he never loses sight of them either.

This principle holds true for the Christian in his home life too. He keeps constantly before him the ideals of what his home should become. He knows, too, what he personally ought to contribute to his home to make it more nearly reflect Christian ideals. And then constantly he keeps striving to achieve those ideals. He never reaches them. He fails again and again. But he never loses sight of them either.

Before he can do this, however, he must have some understanding of the high estate in which Christian marriage stands. He must know what he is striving to achieve before he can put forth efforts to achieve it. At this point he turns to his Bible, and he discovers there the vision he must never allow to escape from his view. He finds there rich insights into what Christian marriage is all about. The Bible establishes a threefold purpose for marriage. Genesis, the book of beginnings — including the beginning of the home — delineates these three purposes. Understanding these purposes and grasping their significance is the beginning step in bringing the uniquely Christian contribution to the home.

THREEFOLD PURPOSE OF MARRIAGE

The threefold purpose is as follows:

1. Genesis 2:18 RSV: "Then the Lord God said, It is not good that the man should be alone; I will make him a helper fit for him." — The first and most obvious purpose of marriage is companionship, the man and the woman being partners together in an intimate relationship.

2. Genesis 2:24 RSV: "Therefore a man leaves his father and his mother and cleaves to his wife, and they become one flesh." — The second purpose of marriage listed in Genesis is physical relationships. Whenever the Bible uses the term "one flesh," it means, at least it always includes, the idea of sexual intimacy.

3. Genesis 1:28 RSV: "And God said to them, Be fruitful and multiply, and fill the earth." — Here is the first Scriptural reference to the progeny of marriage. The Bible from cover to cover has much to say about the place of children in the home.

This threefold purpose of marriage we shall unfold in the following chapters: 1. *companionship,* 2. *physical intimacy,* and 3. the *procreation of children.* It is important that we understand that each of these purposes stands by itself. While all three are interrelated, none of them is dependent for its existence in marriage on the others.

Marriage is for mutual companionship. This is a distinct and unique purpose of marriage.

Marriage is established also with sexual relationships as a conjugal right and marital privilege. These physical relationships have a purpose apart from having children. They stand as one of the purposes of marriage, even when children are left out of consideration.

The third purpose of marriage is for children, a blessing which God bestows upon a couple that has grown together through the intimacy of all their relationships.

It is important to understand these interrelated, yet independent, purposes of marriage. If one were to envision sex as having valid purpose only for the procreation of children, or if one were to place the procreation of children before physical relationships in importance, the place of sex in marriage would be altogether different, and the concept of the threefold purpose of marriage would also be altered. This will become increasingly clear as we develop the thought further.

In the next five chapters we shall concern ourselves with the first purpose of marriage — that of companionship — examining it from various angles. We devote more attention to this purpose of marriage than to either of the others, because *this purpose is basic.* Thoroughly understanding what is involved in making adjustments in the area of interpersonal living establishes the foundation upon which it is relatively easy to build and to make adjustments in sex and to children.

MAN AND WOMAN MADE FOR EACH OTHER

"It is not good that the man should be alone. I will make him a helper fit for him" (Genesis 2:18 RSV). This means that God made the man and the woman for each other.

Paul says, "The wife does not rule over her own body, but

the husband does; likewise the husband does not rule over his own body, but the wife does" (1 Corinthians 7:4 RSV). They are different from each other, physically, emotionally, psychologically. A husband who wishes that his wife were more as he would like her to be, or a wife who wishes that her husband were more as she would like him to be, misses, partially at least, an important point. They were never meant to be the same. They were made to form a "team," to complement each other, to complete each other, to understand each other, and to correlate their individualities so that they might develop a closeness and a unity in the marital bond.

This closeness of unified companionship is something that must be developed. It is not present at the beginning of marriage in the measure that it ought to be present as the marriage develops. It involves a growing process. Day by day, as husband and wife together work consciously at achieving their intellectual, social, and economic adjustments, their goal of a mutual accord and deepening unity becomes more and more of a reality.

The Comparison Between Christ and His Church

This bond that is to develop between husband and wife is so close and so beautiful that God compares it to the most sacred relationship that a man could know — that between Christ and the church. In Ephesians Paul says: "Husbands, love your wives even as Christ also loved the church and gave Himself for it" (Ephesians 5:25). . . . "As the church is subject unto Christ, so let the wives be to their own husbands in everything" (Ephesians 5:24). This is meaningful and significant to Christians because they know something of the relationship of Christ to His church and of the church to Christ. This relationship is at the very center of their lives.

HUSBANDS — AS CHRIST LOVED THE CHURCH

Christians understand how Christ loved the church. He loved it with a giving love, a sacrificing love, a serving love. There was nothing, absolutely nothing, that Christ would not do for or give to His church. He lived for it; He died for it. Concern for His own life was entirely secondary. His own comforts, His own interests, His own benefits, His own advantages and "rights" were never of any moment. His one consuming passion was concern for the welfare of, the redemption of, the church which He loved and which He had come to save. Nothing else mattered to Him. That the church did not love Him as she ought was entirely beside the point. It only manifested the more how much she was in need of His love.

Ephesians sets before husbands this ideal as the pattern they are to emulate in their relationships with their wives. That is a big order. No one can begin to approach the purity of the love of Christ for His church. But that is the ideal toward which all Christian husbands are enjoined to strive. "Husbands, love your wives even as Christ also loved the church" (Ephesians 5:25). Husbands are to love their wives with a giving love, a serving love, a sacrificing love, an unselfish love. Never should they be concerned with their own rights, their own prerogatives, their own comforts and well-being. Their only concern must always be the welfare, the happiness, the good of the woman to whom they are married and whom they love. If they say that they love their wives, they prove the sincerity of that love in the degree to which they become absolutely and completely selfless.

This is the ideal. The husband does not exist who has

reached it or even come close to reaching it. But the Christian husband has never existed who did not constantly *try* to reach it and strive to get closer to it.

WIVES — AS THE CHURCH LOVES CHRIST

The relationship of the wife to her husband is compared in Ephesians 5 with that of the church to Christ. This comparison is consistent with Biblical analyses. Throughout Scripture the church is often referred to as the bride of Christ (2 Corinthians 11:2; Revelation 19:7), and Christ is often spoken of as the Bridegroom (Matthew 9:15; Matthew 25:1; John 3:29; Revelation 21:2). Christians know something about that relationship because they are the church and they love Christ. They show their love for Christ by serving Christ, by obeying Christ, by doing what pleases Christ. Their will is unimportant, because they have submitted their will to Christ's will. Christ's way, Christ's desires have become their own. In Christ they have become completely transformed creatures. This "bondage" to Christ is not by coercion. Christians give themselves over to Christ, commit themselves to Him body and soul, not because they have to, not because they are forced to, but because they want to. It is a service and obedience of love. They know that it is of the very essence of love to do what pleases the one they love. And they have discovered in this bondage to Christ the most wonderful kind of freedom that there is.

Wives are to love their husbands as the church loves Christ. Their love is to be a giving love, a serving love, an obedient love. They are always to be concerned with what pleases their husband, thinking always about the things he would like, that would serve his interests, his desires, his welfare, and the promotion of his work.

THE OBEDIENCE OF LOVE

"Wives, submit yourselves unto your own husbands as unto the Lord. For the husband is the head of the wife, even as Christ is the Head of the church. . . . Therefore as the church is subject unto Christ, so let the wives be to their own husbands in everything" (Ephesians 5:22-24). This passage is sometimes disturbing to wives. The idea of "submitting" themselves seems to be much too strong, and they do not like the inclusion of the word "obey" in the bridal vow of the traditional marriage ceremonies. They object to it because it seems to suggest that they arbitrarily be subject to their husbands in everything. If this were the case, then their objection would be absolutely valid. But such intent is never contained in the word "submit" in the Christian framework.

It is interesting to note that the Greek word that is translated "submit" in the passage "Wives, submit yourselves unto your own husbands" (Ephesians 5:22) is the same word used in the preceding verse when, speaking to Christians generally, Paul says, "Give thanks always for all things unto God and the Father in the name of our Lord Jesus Christ, *submitting* yourselves one to another in the fear of God" (Ephesians 5: 20, 21). This same word is used in 1 Peter 5:5, where young people are urged to respect their elders, "Ye younger, *submit* yourselves unto the elder." It is used also in James 4:7 in describing the Christian's giving himself over to God, "*Submit* yourselves therefore to God." In all instances the word is used, not to express "arbitrary submission," but always "willing commitment."

So also in marriage the concept of "obedience" can be understood only within the context of marital love. This "obedience," this "submission" is never one of servility, but always one of freedom; not one of compulsion, but one of free will. It establishes a role wherein the husband is declared "the head of the wife" (Ephesians 5:23). This is expressed by Paul's own summary of the matter: "Let every one of you in particular so love his wife even as himself, and the wife see that she reverence her husband." (Ephesians 5:33)

THE HEAD OF THE FAMILY

The New Testament, when speaking of the husband, makes his being "head of the wife" a *responsibility* more than a prerogative. It was Joseph, rather than Mary, who had the responsibility for the life of the Infant Jesus when fleeing to Egypt (Matthew 2:13, 14, 20). Though he was not the natural father, and although the responsibility for Jesus' birth, humanly speaking, was Mary's, not his, yet Joseph, as the "head of the family," was responsible for His care. We note, too, that it is to the fathers that the admonition is given to "rear them [their children] in the nurture and admonition of the Lord" (Ephesians 6:4; Colossians 3:21). This means that the husband is responsible for taking over the headship of the home.

The New Testament concept of the marriage relationship and the headship of the husband suggests, not subordination of the wife, but an unselfish, outgoing love on her part, making for a relationship that the Latins would call *primus inter pares,* first among equals. Perhaps in our twentieth century we might understand an analogy between a husband and the chairman of a board of directors. Every organization, no matter how democratic, must lean naturally to a recognized leadership and to someone in whom responsibility is vested. In the home the husband is that person.

It is significant to note, too, that Paul never speaks to

husbands to say to them, "Husbands, your wives must be obedient to you; you are the head and you must stand on your rights." The Christian concept of love would forbid such an attitude on the part of the husband. Paul is always speaking to wives who willingly and out of the response of love are to look to their husbands for the leadership role. It is never a case of the husband demanding; it is rather always a matter of the wife's giving.

It is interesting to note, too, that whenever the New Testament speaks of the roles of husbands and wives in rather sharp distinction, it also adds qualifications. When, for example, Paul makes the rather curt statement, "Neither was the man created for the woman, but the woman for the man" (1 Corinthians 11:9), it might seem that he gives the impression that the only reason for woman's existence is service to her husband. But a few verses later Paul amplifies by saying, "Nevertheless neither is the man without the woman, neither the woman without the man, in the Lord. For as the woman is of the man, even so is the man also by the woman; but all things of God" (1 Corinthians 11:11, 12). Here the basic principle that applies to all Christians becomes specific in its application to husbands and wives. They are "subject to one another out of reverence for Christ." (Ephesians 5:21 RSV)

The Scriptural concept then is that the husband is the head of the home as Christ is the Head of the church, and as the church is obedient to Christ in a response of love, so the wife is to be obedient to her husband in a response of love. The more nearly that these roles can be delineated in a relationship of love, the more nearly both husband and wife will find their complete happiness and fulfillment in their specific roles in the home. Even in twentieth-century

America, where the emancipation of women has brought about a greater equality of sexes, many are raising loud voices deploring the fact that American homes are weakened because husbands are no longer assuming the headship roles that they should. Husbands are being reminded that their wives really do not want equality nearly as much as they want security. Many women are saying publicly that they do not want "partners" in marriage as much as they want "husbands." They want someone whom they can respect and on whom they can depend, someone who will assume responsibility for taking the lead and for making decisions.

THE COMPLETENESS OF CHRISTIAN LOVE

The husband loving his wife as Christ loved the church and the wife loving her husband as the church loves Christ — both of these loves are necessary to make home happiness complete. If one or the other spouse does not give himself fully in an unselfish outgoing love to the other, then the circle of love in that home is broken and happiness cannot be as complete as it should be. If, for example, the husband loves his wife with a giving love, an unselfish love, a serving love, and is constantly putting forth his best efforts to reach that ideal, but she in turn is faultfinding and selfish and demanding and complaining, then the circle of happiness can never be complete. If, on the other hand, the wife loves her husband with a sacrificing, giving, obedient love, and is constantly striving to put that ideal into practice, but her husband is demanding, selfish, thoughtless, concerned only with himself, then again the circle is broken and home happiness cannot be complete. The greatest happiness in the Christian home comes when each, thoughtless of himself and concerned only about the other, strives constantly to reach the Christian ideal. Then literally they will be trying to outdo each other in providing for the happiness of their spouse.

While we are comparing marital love to the relationship of Christ to His church, we must not overlook the nature of Christ's love. "Herein is love, not that we loved God, but that He loved us and sent His Son . . ." (1 John 4:10). Christ loves us not because we are lovable. He loves us in spite of the fact that we are not lovable, in spite of the fact that we do not do what pleases Him, that we do not keep His commands and fulfill His wishes, that we do not live up to what He expects of us. The criterion of His love for us is not anything in us. It is something in God. "God is Love." (1 John 4:8)

This is to be the nature of our love too. Whether or not our spouse is worthy of our love, whether or not he is unlovable and spiteful and difficult to live with is entirely beside the point. Christian love reaches out to the spouse with a love that has responded to the love of God *(agape)*, rather than with a love that responds to the lovability of the spouse *(eros)*. The Christian concept of love *(agape)* is a love that loves no matter what the reaction and the behavior of the person loved might be. His lovableness or unlovableness has nothing to do with it.

Spouses Are a Part of Each Other

Paul gives another vital and significant concept of marriage when he says, "He that loveth his wife loveth himself" (Ephesians 5:28). This concept has profound implications. Husbands and wives often think of their spouses as the other partner in marriage. They think of themselves as two individuals who have contracted to live together as man and wife, each a completely separate entity with his own rights, privileges, and desires.

Paul's concept goes far beyond that. He feels very strongly that the marriage state is a unity. From his way of looking at things there are not two individuals constituting a marriage; rather, each individual is a part of the other. Instead of being two separate individuals they are two parts of one unit, each of which is necessary to make the unity complete. In marriage there is a "one flesh" relationship, and married people are "therefore no more twain, but one flesh" (Matthew 19:6). One's wife is really not the "other" in marriage; she is her husband's "other self," his *alter ego* — inseparably bound and tied to him in love. One's husband is really not the "other" in marriage; he is his wife's "other self," her *altera ego* — inseparably bound and tied to her in love. Therefore when the husband loves his wife, he is not loving another person at all. He is loving a part of himself. When the wife loves her husband, she is not loving another person. She is loving a part of herself.

This concept of unity must mean also that whatever happens to one of the partners happens also to the other. When the husband succeeds in his vocation, the wife is also succeeding, not only because she is standing at his side as his "helpmeet," but also because she is a part of him. They are in his business together. When he fails in his business, she is a part of that failure. His joys are her joys, and his sorrows her sorrows. The reverse is also true. Whatever happens to the wife happens also to the husband. When she has had a particularly rewarding day, her experiences become his, not simply because as an understanding husband he should be interested, but because his wife is a part of him. When she has had a particular trying day, it is a part of himself that has had that experience, and he shares it and feels it with her.

"He who loveth his wife loveth himself." This is a basic

Christian principle which adds depth and meaning to the marriage relationship.

The basis and motive of all Christian behavior, also in the home, is love, Christian love, a love which, because it is attached vertically to Christ, is able to spread horizontally to those with whom we live. In marriage this love is the bond of unity that brings together two people of differing sexes to live together as one — in a lifetime of shared experiences. This unity is more than merely a unity in theory; it is a unity in fact. It is a unity that should become more firm and wonderful through the experiences of each passing day.

CHAPTER FOUR

Adjusting to Each Other

EACH KNOWS PARTNER AS HE IS

Marriage provides the most intimate human relationship possible. It is impossible in this relationship to mask one's shortcomings and weaknesses for long. The fears and frustrations and inadequacies, the character and personality deficiences, which may be hidden in the more casual interrelationships of life, even to an extent in the courtship period, cannot be hid in the intimacy of home life.

After marriage, spouses sometimes feel that their partners have changed and that they are no longer the same people they were in courtship days. They feel that they have lost their consideration, their thoughtfulness, their kindness, and in general display many more undesirable characteristics than they did before the marriage. This may sometimes be true. People do change. Every person they meet, also their marriage partners, has an influence upon them. But by and large the basic personality pattern of the husband or wife changes very little and very slowly, if at all. Each remains basically the same person that he was before the marriage, with the same strengths and weaknesses that he always had. After marriage, spouses often discover in each other characteristics they did not know were there before, or, what may also be the case, they focus their attention on characteristics different from those they saw before the marriage. The perspective changes when two people begin to share responsibilities.

For this reason a perceptive and intelligent courtship is so essential. It is not enough to follow the dictates of one's heart when selecting a mate with whom to share a life; one must employ also his mind. One must learn to know his partner as fully as possible, to know his goals and ambitions, his reactions and motivations, his likes and dislikes, his individualities, his inclinations, his friends. Love is essential; but just as essential is an intelligent decision based on as many known factors as possible.

Ordinarily when we associate with people whose characteristics irritate us, the solution is easy. We change our associations. In marriage we must turn to other solutions, because we are dealing not with a superficial relationship, but with a permanent relationship in which the tying bond is to be love. Marriage partners must call on all the resources at their command, to react and to adjust to each other in a mature fashion, in a Christian spirit. For the Christian couple it means "proving to each other the sincerity of their love" (2 Corinthians 8:8). Christians do not dwell on the weaknesses and shortcomings of their spouse, but rather, as Luther says in his explanation of the Eighth Commandment, "they defend him, speak well of him, and put the best construction on everything." [1] They learn in the crucible of their everyday experiences that love "covers a multitude of sins" (1 Peter 4:8). They accept each other for what they are, and they manifest toward each other those Christian virtues that St. Paul enjoins: "Put on then, as God's chosen ones, holy and beloved, compassion, kindness, lowliness, meekness, and patience, forbearing one another, and if one has a complaint against another, forgiving each other; as the Lord has forgiven you, so you also must forgive. And above all these put on love, which binds everything together in perfect harmony" (Colossians 3:12-14 RSV). Love, genuine Christian love, should always be the mark of the Christian's attitude, including his attitude toward the weaknesses in his spouse.

DID I MARRY THE RIGHT PARTNER?

Sometimes couples, after they have settled down to the realities of life, feel, consciously or subconsciously, that they could have found greater marital happiness with a different spouse. This may in some instances be true. Certainly it is not true that there is just one man and one woman on this earth who are meant for each other and who alone can find happiness with each other. There are thousands of men or women with whom one could live happily in marriage.[2] But

[1] "Thou shalt not bear false witness against thy neighbor." (Exodus 20:16)

[2] Christians, of course, believe in divine providence. Also in marriage they believe that God has directed their lives and led them to each other. However, interpreting Matthew 19:6: "What God has joined together, let not man put asunder," to mean that individual "marriages are made in heaven," that God has selected just one person to be our partner, does not convey what the passage says. This passage refers rather to the institution of marriage, which is established by God, and therefore is not to be put asunder. It means that once a man and woman have joined themselves together in holy wedlock, which has been ordained by God, no man should break it up.

this is completely beside the point. The fact of the matter is that the couple is married to each other and no one else is involved. They need to concentrate their best efforts in building this estate that they have established and give their energies to their own relationship.

Mature people understand how impossible it is to compare one person with another. They know that when they look at other men or women, or other people's husbands or wives, they are seeing them for the most part in their better moments and better moods. They certainly are not seeing the total persons as one comes to know them in marriage. They are not sharing with them the little day-by-day responsibilities and the irritating frustrations that life together can bring about. They see only a segment of those people's personalities — as they react in certain situations at certain times. The result is that they compare the weaknesses of their spouse with the strong points of someone else, and the spouse may come out second best in the comparison. This is not fair. It is true, of course, that every other person will have many desirable characteristics that one's spouse does not have and that the spouse has weaknesses that other people do not have. But it is also true that the spouse has good points that the other person does not have and that the other person, if he were known more intimately, would be shown to have weaknesses that the spouse does not have. Hence Christians, rather than compare their spouses unfavorably with someone else, should in love appreciate their good qualities and in love also forgive their weaknesses.

INCOMPATIBILITIES

The word "incompatibility" is commonly used whenever personality tensions and conflicts are present. There certainly are instances of deep-seated incompatibility, where husbands and wives are so completely different from each other that they seem to have no common meeting ground. But the instances of absolute incompatibility in marriage are rare. Most often the basic problem is not one of incompatibility. It is rather one of immaturity, of selfishness and self-centeredness, of unwillingness or inability to work together and to spend the effort in understanding each other and making the necessary compromises. Every marriage, without exception, is incompatible. As Chesterton said, "I have known many happy marriages, but never a compatible one." [3] *Marriage is the lifelong process of working out the incompatibilities.* There are problems and difficulties in every marriage. That problems exist is not an indication that the home life is undesirable or that couples are unsuited for each other. What is important is how those problems are handled. What is done with them determines how successful the marriage is.

When difficulties in marital adjustments occur, each individual does well to look first to himself, rather than to his partner, for the blame. No one is perfect, and the inability to adjust to imperfections is always an indication of a lack of maturity or spirituality. Marital adjustments would be much easier if everyone concerned concentrated more on *being* the right partner than in *having* the right partner. Paul says, "Brethren, if a man is overtaken in any trespass, you who are spiritual should restore him in a spirit of gentleness. Look to yourself, lest you, too, be tempted. . . . Let each one test his own work, and then his reason to boast will be in himself alone and not in his neighbor. For each man will have to bear his own load." (Galatians 6:1, 4, 5 RSV)

I think here of a story that has its application to marriage

[3] Quoted in Trueblood, op. cit., p. 51.

too. A man was contemplating a move to a new community. In an advance visit he asked a clerk in a community store whether the people in the town were friendly and thoughtful. The clerk asked him what the people were like in the community he was leaving. The newcomer replied that they were rather indifferent and not to his liking. The clerk then replied, "You'll find them the same here." Our difficulties in adjustment are often caused more by ourselves than by others — also in marriage.

MANY ADJUSTMENTS AND COMPROMISES

Marriage calls for many adjustments on the part of both husband and wife. From the purely physical point of view the wife is usually required to make more dramatic changes in her way of life. In his book *Making Your Marriage Succeed,* Theodore Adams has an excellent section dealing with some of these adjustments. He says: "The wife will probably have to make more adjustments than the husband because her life is more centered in the home. She takes his name instead of her own. She changes her place of residence, not only from her parental home, but perhaps to a place far distant. She must leave the security of her former home for a new security that she and her husband must build for themselves. She has to change her role in life to the manifold duties of housekeeper, homemaker, business manager, nurse, companion, cook, and sweetheart. To do all this requires adjustment in her way of life and thought." [4]

Husbands must make many adjustments too. They must learn what it means to share a life. They are no longer independent to do what they please as they please. Other

[4] Theodore Adams, *Making Your Marriage Succeed* (New York: Harper and Brothers, 1953), pp. 93, 94.

people must fit into their schedules. Becoming a husband means assuming a new role for which new aptitudes need to be developed. Money and its spending, interests, hobbies must be shared, sometimes changed.

Both husband and wife have many adjustments to make to each other. Adams says about this: "You need to learn to respect each other's likes and dislikes as to food and clothes, amusements and ways of housekeeping. You will do well to understand and recognize each other's moods, to know when to speak and when to keep quiet, to recognize that there are special times of tension when one or both are tired and weary and more inclined to be irritable. You have to learn to understand, and to trust when you cannot quite understand." [5]

Interpersonal relationships and interpersonal living always call for many compromises. Each must be ready to give and to take, to give up and to "give in." This is true wherever two or more people live together. Wherever there are two or more persons living or working together, thoughtfulness demands that each adjust to the other to maintain a satisfactory relationship.

This principle is true not only in the major adjustments, but also, yes, especially, in the little day-by-day incidents of living together. Every married couple could illustrate this by scores of examples. Let me mention but two.

I know of one couple where the husband loves to play golf. The wife loathes it. She on the other hand loves to dance, and he loathes dancing. This couple wants to do as many things together as possible. They talk it out and agree to take up bowling together. This does not mean that hus-

[5] Adams, p. 96.

bands should give up golf or that bowling is the solution
for the recreation needs of the family. (I know of some
families who have taken up golf because it is one sport that
husband and wife can enjoy together even in old age.) This
is merely an illustration of how the principle of compromise
is essential in family relationships. Here is another from my
own home. Before we were married, my wife liked black
coffee, but she preferred it lukewarm. My tastes leaned to
piping-hot coffee with cream. Now we both enjoy piping-hot
black coffee, and we would drink it no other way. Each
learned really to enjoy something the other preferred.

This principle of compromise and adjustment shapes the
pattern of the couple's entire life together. The family interests depend upon what the interests of the individuals in
the family are and upon the adaptation that each makes of
his own interests with those of the other. Thus one family
might become very interested in athletics or music or litera-
ture, while another family is not interested in them at all.
One family might do housework together, while another family
works out another pattern. One couple might sleep late,
while another are early risers. The important thing is that
each in his own situation, in conformity with the likes and
dislikes of the other, comes to the solution that is satisfactory
to both.

As these compromises are made, as the interests of the
one gradually become the interests of the other, the unity
of companionship between husband and wife continues to
grow, and eventually each even begins to become somewhat
like the other in likes and dislikes. This shows itself in the
food they eat, in the clothing they wear, in the cars they
drive. In most instances I am certain that if a husband and
wife had gone their separate ways before marriage to choose,

let us say, furniture for their living room, their selection would be entirely different. If, however, after fifteen years of adjustments and compromises in married life they were to go out on the same errand, the chances are good that the selection of each would be quite similar to that of the other.. Even their tastes and their interests grow into a unity.

THE LITTLE DAILY ADJUSTMENTS ARE IMPORTANT

Most often the areas of interpersonal living that cause the greatest difficulties are the little, ordinary, day-by-day experiences. It is a peculiar trait of human nature that when we have major crises or tragedies to face, we summon the necessary resources to face and bear them. But the insignificant ones, those which, comparatively speaking, ought to cause hardly a ripple, sometimes tear us all apart. I have, for example, seen a woman stand bravely by as she watched her house burn to the ground. Her reaction was one of strong Christian faith and submission to the ways of God. And I have seen that same woman go all to pieces when she lost a single glove, or when her child, in trying to be helpful with the dishes, broke a glass.

In many marriages spouses are ready to stand by each other through all the major problems and character weaknesses. Sometimes they will remain loyal even through crime and adultery and drunkenness or other gross social sins. But in the little day-by-day adjustments, in the little personality weaknesses that are of minor moment, they nag and irritate each other mercilessly. I remember one husband complaining about his wife. There was nothing of major importance that was pulling them apart. Those things they had settled. But he became very emotional as he pounded his fist on my desk and said, "It even gripes me the way she eats potato chips."

In married life couples ought to pray often to be big-enough Christians to overlook the petty and insignificant. People often are big enough to overlook the big, but too little to overlook the little. Every Christian's prayer again and again must be, "God, make me big enough to overlook little things."

LEARN TO TALK THINGS THROUGH

One of the first things that a husband and wife must learn is to talk things through together. One would think that to do this would be very easy for two people who love each other. But many couples have never learned to do this even after years of married life. That they have lived together for many years does not mean that they have strengthened their communication with each other. The ability to communicate grows and develops. So does lack of communication. In human relationships emotions are always involved. Unless we increasingly learn to see "eye to eye," we increasingly find ourselves talking "at" each other or "past" each other, without any mutual understanding.

So often people view problems or situations from their own particular point of view, and they never are able to get through, or do not want to get through, to understand the viewpoint of the other or to adjust to the viewpoint of the other.

I remember well one couple who had been married for twenty-five years. Problems with them had reached such a climactic pitch that by the time they reached me the husband and the wife were not able even to talk to each other calmly. Whenever the husband wanted to speak, I had to ask him to speak to me, and whenever the wife had something to say, she had to do likewise. Neither could speak to the other without becoming angry and without bringing all types of skeletons from the closet.

Every problem, every incident, every experience can always be viewed from several points of view. Every person looks at any incident out of the frame of reference of his own personality, his own background, his own needs, and his own thought patterns. As a house or a tree or a body looks different from various perspectives, so ordinary events, innocent in themselves, look entirely different from different points of view. What is meant one way can very easily be interpreted another way because the words used conjure up different images to different people. The same incident will evoke different reactions from the various people who are experiencing it. As a political candidate may make a statement which seems to have almost the opposite meaning to a Republican that it does to a Democrat, depending upon his point of view, so the same thing can and does happen frequently in family relationships. No person is so completely objective that he can calmly and unemotionally view every word that is spoken and every deed that is done. Marriage partners, too, evaluate, think about, and most important of all, judge each other's words and actions in the light of their past experiences together.

Each individual is aware of how he feels and reacts to a particular situation, and sometimes he takes for granted that his spouse feels and reacts in the same way he does. But he may be seriously mistaken. Hence it is of extreme importance that couples learn early to listen as well as to speak, to try to understand what the spouse is thinking and feeling, and as much as possible, to sympathize with the reactions. It is only as people "get inside each other," only as they try to stand where the spouse is standing and to view the situation from his vantage point, that they can really understand each other. It is absolutely essential that they do this if they are to achieve the unity of mutually understanding each other.

Seeking Help from a Third Person

There are times in every couple's home life when it would be well for them to seek the help of a third party with whom to discuss some of their problems. Scripture reminds us to "bear one another's burdens" (Galatians 6:2 RSV), to help each other share the loads we carry.

Usually when adjustment problems arise it is not so much the problem itself as the way the individuals look at the problem that causes difficulty. Generally it is not a matter of one's being right and the other's being wrong. In the emotional involvement of marriage, husbands and wives often feel that they must defend their viewpoints, that they must maintain their own pride and self-respect, or they cannot understand what makes their mate think as he does, and thus they like to assume for themselves that they are entirely in the right and their spouse is entirely in the wrong. The difficulty is usually due to the perspective, each viewing the problem from a different point of view. Because each looks at the given situation only from where he stands, he finds it difficult and sometimes impossible to see it from where his spouse stands.

The third person becomes one who sees the problem from "neither" point of view, but from a "disinterested" point of view. He is not emotionally involved in the problem, and hence his feelings do not complicate the matter. He is able to point out to the couple the varying points of view. Once a problem is brought out into the open and seen objectively from all sides, once each person sees the problem as the other sees it, it takes on an altogether different hue. This third person may be a trusted friend, a pastor, a doctor, a marriage counselor, some capable person in whom the couple has confidence. If at all possible, too, it is well if the person is a Christian with an understanding of the Christian concept and purpose of marriage.

Above all, couples should never be ashamed to approach such a person with their problems. Too much is at stake to let pride stand in the way of securing help. Often they feel that it is a disgrace or an admission of failure on their part to have to resort to an outside person. They feel that they should be able to handle their problems by themselves. The fact of the matter is that for every person there are times when his problems become too large for him to handle.

Most pastors have premarital discussions with young couples about to be married. They usually emphasize how important it is that young couples seek advice as soon as they have their first adjustment problem. In my personal experience I always stress with these young people that it doesn't matter how minor the difficulty might be. It may be over a piece of burned toast or over a fifty-cent piece.

The size of the problem is unimportant, but *how they make adjustments to it is extremely important.* If these people can learn through the experience of the burned toast to talk things through, to express themselves openly and freely, and to get through to each other, then they have grown and have moved one step closer to adequate solutions for future problems. If they learn to do this early in their lives, and continue to do it through all of their experiences together, then they will have learned an important lesson for marital happiness. If they do not learn this early in their marital life, if they do not from the very beginning talk through their differences and difficulties, then these differences will continue to mount and, what is even worse, will remain locked up inside them. And the more they mount and store up, the more difficult it becomes to discuss them freely. What happens then is that these resentments become so involved that a tremendous mountain of negative emotion builds up. This may all lie dormant until a minor crisis arises. Then all of the pent-up emotion blows out, and neither is rational enough to discuss matters as they ought to be discussed. The minor crisis becomes magnified out of all proportion. On the other hand, as each learns to make adjustments to his partner, he learns to understand and appreciate the thought pattern of the one with whom he is living, and thus the unity continues to deepen and grow.

That couple is fortunate and on the road to good marital adjustment which has resolved, and which carries out, the determination never to allow anything that disturbs them to remain unspoken, no matter how insignificant it may seem. Much better that one's emotions come out into the open and be aired, even though feelings might be ruffled for a brief time, than to have a major explosion create major difficulties later. I would much rather have a thousand firecrackers explode over a period of ten years than to have one huge bomb fall on my house at the end of the ten years. Firecrackers would do much less damage.

Growing Unity Through Adjustments

It is in the ordinary day-by-day adjustments that love and unity grow. In the closeness of intimate sharing the bonds deepen. With each succeeding day the joys that each of the married partners experiences are doubled because there are two to share and enjoy them. At the same time all sorrows and burdens are cut in half and made easier to bear because there are two to carry and share them. God said, "It is not good that the man should be alone" (Genesis 2:18). One of our country's leading experts on family relationships puts it this way: "True love between a man and a woman may be defined as a relationship in which each helps to preserve and enlarge the life of the other. . . . It knows that each can fulfill his own destiny only by collaborative effort with the other in carrying out life's immemorial design. Mature love thrives therefore on a realistic basis of equal exchange which sets up a benign circle of mutual pleasure, reassurance, and inspiration." [6]

St. Paul's exhortation to the Christian's general conduct applies with equal force to his conduct in his home:

> For you were called to freedom, brethren; only do not use your freedom as an opportunity for the flesh, but through love be servants of one another. For the whole Law is fulfilled in one word, "You shall love your neighbor [spouse] as yourself!" But if you bite and devour one another, take heed that you are not consumed by one another.
>
> But I say, walk by the Spirit, and do not gratify the desires of the flesh. . . . The fruit of the Spirit is love, joy, peace, patience, kindness, goodness, faithfulness, gentleness, self-control; against such there is no law. And those who belong to Christ Jesus have crucified the flesh with its passions and desires.
>
> If we live by the Spirit, let us also walk by the Spirit. Let us have no self-conceit, no provoking of one another, no envy of one another. (Galatians 5:13-16, 22-25 RSV)

[6] Smiley Blanton, *Love or Perish* (New York: Simon and Schuster, 1956), p. 86.

CHAPTER FIVE

Growing into a Unity

In the process of living together and growing together there often, yes, always, is a vast gulf between what a marriage ought to be and what it actually is. This is because, as we have said before, Christians are constantly in the state of "becoming," constantly moving toward the goal of spiritual maturation. They are, and they will always continue to be, "frail and sinful" human beings. If these frailties could exist in a vacuum, if one's weaknesses could be the concern of the individual alone, there would be no problem. But that is never the case.

Human beings are also social beings, and whatever is a part of them affects everyone with whom they come into contact. The man with a quick temper, for example, or a biting tongue, or a self-centered personality always displays those characteristics to the people about him. And of course, those to whom these characteristics become most evident, and who are most immediately and deeply affected by them, are the people with whom he lives most closely in his own family circle. They see him most nearly as he really is as a total person. They see every side of his personality, both desirable and undesirable. A husband, for example, who is consistently smiling and generous and thoughtful of his help in the office may be churlish and hard to please at home. The salesman who finds it easy, because of the nature of his work, to speak readily to people with whom he deals may be uncommunicative in his family circle. The wife who is a picture of graciousness to guests may be complaining and sarcastic much of the time with her husband; the woman who is known widely to be an understanding person may be nagging and faultfinding with the man she loves.

SPOUSES SHOULD FEEL FREE WITH EACH OTHER

The process of living together day by day makes it easier for people to be "natural" with one another, for them to let down all psychological guards. While other people might not understand them fully, or might misinterpret what they say and how they act, they like to assume that their spouses do understand them and accept them the way they are. And so the worst as well as the best in people comes to the fore as they relax and become truly themselves, disrobed of the front they need constantly put up for the outside world.

Unfortunately though, as a spouse releases the tensions and irritations that have built up within him, his marriage partner is at the receiving end, even though she is not responsible for them. She, too, has emotions, and they react to the behavior. Many a wife knows that her husband, after spending a day of supposed calm self-assurance in the office, pulls out all the stops of irritability when he reaches home. His secretary admires his composure, and his community regards him as an unselfish, hard-working asset. But they never see him in the moods in which his wife sees him! Many a husband knows, too, that his wife, after a particularly harassing day with the children, or after some of her plans were upset, is completely out of sorts and short-tempered. Everyone tells him what a pretty wife he has and how sweet and thoughtful she is. But they never see her as he sometimes sees her in the home! Every husband and every wife experience this in greater or lesser degree.

In a sense this is good. The home should be the place where husband and wife can be free enough to express in some way their deepest emotions. Every person, no matter who he is, needs to have a safety valve to release some of the pressures that build up within him. His home should provide him with such a valve. Furthermore, his home should manifest the kind of atmosphere where he can be himself, freely, without inhibition, where he can express entirely and exactly how he feels, and where he can be sure that through it all he has the understanding of his spouse. No responsible person, and certainly no Christian person, will be unbridled in his emotional outbursts. His personality is disciplined, and even though he feels free to express his deepest emotions, he is careful to give vent to his feelings in the least destructive way. Scripture always admonishes us to live in Christian graces, which include "patience, kindness . . . gentleness, self-control." (Galatians 5:22, 23)

EMOTIONAL RELEASES AFFECT THE ATMOSPHERE OF THE HOME

His emotional releases influence and affect the atmosphere of the home. Hasty words, unkind gestures and remarks, selfish emotional tantrums cut deeply and leave their impressions, sometimes for a lifetime. Everyone has experienced over and over again that remarks he once made under stress, remarks which in his saner moments he never would have made, and which he soon forgets, continue to linger and fester many years later in the person to whom they were directed.

As they grow in their Christian life, Christians must become increasingly aware of two considerations in this connection.

They will first of all be sure to manifest enough consistent Christian love to forgive and forget all hurts that come their way from their spouses. Eliminating grudges is one of the characteristics of a Christian personality. No Christian in any capacity can for long carry about deep-seated resentments and still remain a healthy, happy Christian person. Certainly this is true in the home. Unless his heart is entirely "without guile," (Psalm 32:2; 1 Peter 2:22), unless he is "pure in heart" (Matthew 5:8), free from emotional barriers and tensions, he cannot contribute as unqualifiedly as he should to the total happiness of the home.

Then, too, every Christian will strive to be mature enough to understand that when upsets and emotional aberrations do occur, the irritation displayed and apparently directed at the spouse or the particular situation of the moment is actually a result of the irritation that has built up by completely unrelated experiences. The immediate circumstance is merely the occasion that provides the outlet for the tensions that were already there. When, for example, a husband seems out of sorts and unusually impatient, even harsh in his judgments of matters of minor significance, the family may find it difficult to understand why he is making a mountain out of a mole hill. But his emotional reaction to the immediate situation may have its real cause in the trying and exhausting day he had at the office. Had his day been different, what irritates him would be laughed off under other circumstances. If the wife seems unusually sarcastic or pessimistic, it may very well not be because of the relatively minor mistake that her husband made but rather a release of the tensions that have been building up in her all day. Understanding the deeper behavior motivations in our spouses makes us understand that not all negative reaction can be interpreted personally. Much of it is simply emotional release, for which there should be place in every marriage.

CHRISTIANITY INFLUENCES ALSO EMOTIONS

There is, however, also another side of the picture. Christianity involves a great deal more than merely observing a few forms or refraining from some of the coarser social sins or giving intellectual assent to a particular set of doctrines. Christianity always involves a living relationship with Christ, a relationship which makes one a new creature. "If any man be in Christ, he is a new creature; old things are passed away; behold, all things are become new" (2 Corinthians 5:17). This new relationship affects his personality and in a growing measure results in a life of Christian virtues and Christian graces. As he tries to become more consistent in his Christian living, he attempts under every circumstance and in every situation to manifest those virtues to which he pays lip service: understanding, patience, love, unselfishness, liberality, kindness, a forgiving spirit. He understands that those are virtues not only to be talked about, but to be lived. The home provides a wonderful opportunity, a marvelous laboratory, to put them into practice.

Peter talks about this in his epistle. "You wives, be submissive to your husbands. . . . Let not yours be the outward adorning with braiding of hair, decoration of gold, and wearing of robes, but let it be the hidden person of the heart with the imperishable jewel of a gentle and quiet spirit, which in God's sight is very precious. . . . Likewise you husbands, live considerately with your wives, bestowing honor on the woman as the weaker sex, since you are joint heirs of the grace of life, in order that your prayers may not be hindered. Finally, all of you, have unity of spirit, sympathy, love of the brethren, a tender heart and a humble mind. Do not return evil for evil or reviling for reviling; but on the contrary bless, for to this you have been called, that you may obtain a blessing. For 'He that would love life and see good days, let him keep his tongue from evil and his lips from speaking guile; let him turn away from evil and do right; let him seek peace and pursue it.'" (1 Peter 3:1, 3, 4, 7-11 RSV)

This is not always easy to carry out. But there would be no virtue in any personality trait if no effort were involved in developing and practicing it. There is no virtue, for example, in being understanding of another person's actions when that person's behavior is in full accord with what we should like to have him do. There is real virtue, however, when we seek to understand and to be kind and considerate in our judgments when the behavior of the individual is beyond our comprehension.

There is no virtue in being patient when there is nothing in a situation to try our patience. But when everything seems to be going wrong, when circumstances are nearly unendurable, when we are "ready to tear our hair," if then we remain patient, we are practicing a virtue.

There is no particular virtue in loving those people who are lovable to us. That is only a natural reaction, and as Jesus said, "even the publicans do that " (Matthew 5:46). The real virtue of love shows itself when we love people who are not loving and lovable, even hateful and despicable. That is when love is really love.

This is what Jesus said. "For if you love those who love you, what reward have you? Do not even the tax collectors do the same? And if you salute only your brethren, what more are you doing than others? Do not even the Gentiles do the same?" (Matthew 5:46, 47 RSV)

Christian virtues don't "just happen." Developing them takes effort and struggle against our natural inner reactions. St. Paul always looked at the Christian life as a struggle. Listen to him as he lays bare his soul to tell of his own inner spiritual struggle. "The good that I would I do not, but the evil which I would not, that I do" (Romans 7:19). He compares the Christian life to a wrestling match, saying, "We wrestle not against flesh and blood, but against principalities, against powers" (Ephesians 6:12). Again and again he tells us that "the flesh lusteth against the spirit, and the spirit against the flesh, and these are contrary the one to the other" (Galatians 5:17). He reminds us to take up our battle with "the whole armor of God" (Ephesians 6:11). He urges Timothy to "fight the good fight of faith." (1 Timothy 6:12)

The Christians life is always an intense personal struggle between the forces of good and the forces of evil, a battle that will continue till the end of life itself.

There is no place like his home for the Christian to develop and practice these virtues.

Somewhere I read the following "Ten Commandments for Husbands and Wives." They are worth repeating. It would be well for every husband and wife to read them to each other often and to vow to live according to them:

Ten Commandments for Husbands

1. Thou shalt provide the necessities of life for thy family, and shalt not close thy fist too tightly around thy billfold.
2. Remember that thou must assume some of the responsibility in thy home.
3. Thou shalt share some of thy recreation hours with thy wife and family, remembering that a family which plays together stays together.
4. Thou shalt take thy wife into thy confidence and share thy plans with her, remembering that she is thy partner, not thy hired hand.
5. Thou shalt enter into thy house with cheerfulness and avoid faultfinding and a critical spirit as much as possible.

6. Thou shalt not embarrass or criticize thy wife before thy friends and relatives; nor shalt thou allow anyone to criticize thy wife to thy face and get away with it.

7. Thou shalt not take thy wife for granted, but shalt keep her love in the same way in which thou didst win it.

8. There shall be no one before thy wife except God.

9. Thou shalt live a life of high moral purity.

10. Thou shalt give God a place — yea, first place in thy heart and home.

Ten Commandments for Wives

1. Thou shalt not nag.

2. Thou shalt spend thy husband's money with care and wisdom.

3. Thou shalt keep thy tongue with all diligence, not permitting it to run loose in gossip.

4. Thou shalt not always be comparing thy husband with other men, nor shalt thou continually remind him of all the men thou couldst have married.

5. Thou shalt not be the boss.

6. Thou shalt not be possessed of an excessively jealous spirit.

7. Thou shalt coddle thy husband, doing for him those little things that mean so much.

8. Thou shalt give diligence to keep thyself and thy home attractive, remembering thou must not only win thy husband's love, but also keep it.

9. Thou shalt prize thy womanly virtues and value them more than life itself.

10. Thou shalt have a genuine religion and a deep trust in God.

In his book *Making Your Marriage Succeed,* Adams quotes a list of some very practical suggestions that had been handed to him for both husbands and wives as they start their life together. The list is just as appropriate for husbands and wives celebrating their fiftieth wedding anniversary as it is for young people just beginning their married life. It should have a prominent place on a bulletin board of the home for ready reference.

Never both be angry at once.

Never taunt the other with a past mistake.

Never forget the happy hours of early love.

Never meet without a loving welcome.

Never talk *at* each other, alone or in a crowd.

Never yell at each other unless the house is on fire.

Let each one strive oftenest to yield to the wishes of the other.

Let self-denial be the daily aim and practice of each.

Never let the sun go down on any anger or grievance.

Never allow a reasonable request to have to be made a second time.

Never make a remark in public at the expense of the other. It may seem very funny sometimes, but it hurts.

Never sigh for what might have been, but make the best of what is.

Never find fault unless it is certain that a fault has been committed, and even then, always speak lovingly.

Never part for the day without loving words to think about during the absence. Short words in the morning make a long day.

Never let any fault that you have committed go by until you have confessed it and are forgiven.

Never forget that the nearest approach to heaven on earth is where two souls rival each other in unselfishness.

Never be contented until you know that both of you are walking in the straight and narrow road, each helping the other.

Never forget that marriage is ordained of God and that His
  blessing alone can make it what it ought to be.
Never let your human hopes stop short of the Home Eternal.[1]

To all of these I would add one more. "Never use the
word 'always' " — like: "You *always* lose your temper so
quickly"; "you *always* go on the defensive"; "you *always* leave
your socks on the floor"; "you *always* nag." Or from the negative point of view: "You *never* listen when I talk"; "you *never*
are ready on time." There is no person who is *always* engaged
in his faults or *never* doing what is proper. The words "always" or "never" carry barbs and implications which in themselves are cutting. Not using those little words can change
the tone of a criticism from a destructive one to a construc-
tive one.

I remember one couple who were having unusual adjustment problems. In fact, the wife had already sued for divorce.
Each was quick and sharp of tongue. We met for many counseling sessions. The couple later told me that most helpful
to their relationship was the suggestion to stop using the word
"always." It was the turning point in their marriage.

In addition to this every Christian couple ought to read
together very frequently, and strive to put into practice with
each other, the description of real love from one of the great
chapters of the Bible: "Love is patient and kind; love is not
jealous or boastful; it is not arrogant or rude. Love does not
insist on its own way; it is not irritable or resentful; it does
not rejoice at wrong, but rejoices in the right. Love bears
all things, believes all things, hopes all things, endures all
things." (1 Corinthians 13:4-7 RSV)

[1] Adams, pp. 92, 93.

CHAPTER SIX

Understanding Each Other

Christian Virtues "Other-Directed"

We have said earlier that the virtues that make for a good
Christian also make for a good spouse. The reason for this
is that Christian virtues are always based on Christian love,
and Christian love is always "other-directed." It centers on
the other person and is always concerned with fulfilling the
needs of the other person. The Christian looks "not only to
his own interests, but also to the interests of others" (Philippians 2:4 RSV). The more he grows in his Christian graces,
the more he fills the needs and interests of those with whom
he lives.

Husbands and wives, because of the roles that they assume in their lives together, as well as because of their sex
differences, have differing psychological needs. It is essential
that each spouse understand those needs in order that he
might intelligently apply his principles of love in fulfilling
them.

Husband's Principal Need: Recognition

The husband's principal emotional need is for recognition
and a sense of achievement. As head of the family he feels
responsible for providing his home and caring for its needs.
On the job he is moving in a world of rugged competition
and is constantly seeking status. He encounters many frustrations. His day is filled with problems and discouragements,
and he often feels inadequate to his challenges. He fails to
meet his quota, his employer is dissatisfied, a hoped-for sale
falls through, a competitor takes advantage of him, his help
proves inefficient, his boss is unreasonable.

Moreover, his business or professional life, whatever his

68

job might be, is important to him. It is to this that he devotes the majority of his energies. It is here where he is seeking to advance. To do so means giving of his best in planning and energy, devoting perhaps many long and grueling hours to his work. He feels keenly that it is here that he must succeed if he is to provide status for himself and his family.

To remain fit for this activity, he needs someone to encourage him, to "inspire" and appreciate him, to believe in him, and from time to time to refuel his ego and to remind him "how great he is." More than anything else he needs the feeling that there is someone at home who understands him and who appreciates what he is doing. For this reason it is important that again and again his wife restore his sense of importance and accomplishment. She must reaffirm her appreciation, her loyalty, her devotion, her confidence in him. A woman cannot overestimate what a source of power she is to her husband if she instills in him the feeling that in whatever he is doing she is "with him" and supporting him with her approval and admiration. The kiss or word of encouragement as he leaves for work in the morning lingers with him all day. The hearty welcome when he comes home at night, and the warm and genuine interest and understanding that she shows in his problems and his work when they are together, provide a support to him far beyond what she can even imagine. He will be able to undergo many difficulties and solve many problems simply by the confident assurance that he has a wife who cares and to whom he really matters as a person.

The wife needs to understand that a very important part of her husband's role is his work. This in one sense is his life. But he must have the feeling that his work is not only his, but that in a very important way it is hers too. He feels frustrated if his wife thinks of his work as being in competition with her own interests or her time. He likes to think of her being interested in what he is doing and co-operating and adjusting to whatever rigors his vocation might demand. The wife therefore must think of herself as a partner in her husband's life's endeavor, supplying the fuel that he needs to meet his challenges.

Before promoting executives in business, many companies interview the wives as well as the husbands. They know that the husband's performance will depend a great deal upon the quality of his home life and the attitude that his wife has toward what he is doing. The president of one very successful business firm once told me that one of the greatest deterrents to the advancement of many men was their wives. He expected them to put in overtime when it was needed, to be interested in their work, but they were often undergoing conflict because their wives did not think it right, or fair to them, or they thought their husbands were being treated unjustly. Many wives, he said, wanted their husbands to be successful, but were not ready to make any of the sacrifices that success requires. Thus they, and not their husbands, were at fault for their failure to advance. If a wife is continually showing her disinterest in her husband's work and its problems; if she shows dissatisfaction and self-centered attitudes regarding it; if she is not genuinely proud of the role he is fulfilling in God's world (or if he does not feel that she is proud of it); if she is even constantly nagging him because of the kind of job he holds, or the amount of money he earns, or this or that undesirable factor in his work, she is tearing down his ego and undermining the confidence and sense of importance he needs to achieve the success she so much wants him to have. If she wants to be proud of what he accomplishes and contributes to society, she must first of all be proud of him and support him as he works at it.

Unless the wife, even in moments when she herself is discouraged, remembers her role and tries always to be a source of inspiration and encouragement to her husband, she is not fulfilling everything that she should be in her marriage. She might be an excellent housekeeper, a patient mother with her children, a financial wizard, an efficient nurse, a Hollywood beauty. But if she fails to convince him, because she actually believes it, of his worth and capabilities; if she is not constantly restoring his feelings of being appreciated for all that he is doing; if she does not by all that she says and does show her admiration, her confidence, and her loyalty to him, then she is not fulfilling his principal need. The Christian, as was said earlier, is always engaged in the kind of love that reaches out to the needs of others. For the wife, this must begin with her husband.

WIFE'S PRINCIPAL NEED: AFFECTION AND COMPANIONSHIP

The wife has needs too. One of them is for affection. By and large, women are more sensitive and tender and sympathetic, and often less realistic and logical than men. They want to give themselves to someone, to a person rather than to a cause, and they in turn want someone who needs and cares about them. The predilection of women to be attached to a person rather than to a cause is important to remember if a husband would understand his wife. She is not vitally and essentially interested in his work *for its own sake.* She is interested in it because she is *first of all interested in the person* who is engaged in the work. The husband has been caught up in the challenges of his occupation, had in fact been preparing for them and perhaps even engaged in them before he was married and is therefore interested in them for their own sake. This does not mean that he is not interested in his wife. It only means that he is interested in his work in a way different from what his wife is.

Another of her needs is that of companionship (especially if she has a full-time homemaker's role). Whereas her husband spends hours and days at a time in varying environments with varying challenges, the wife spends most of her time in the home. Even if his job is routine and monotonous, the mere going to work gives him a change of scenery which she does not enjoy. She does not meet with and converse with people as frequently as her husband does. During the day she is not challenged intellectually nearly as much as he. Much of her work is routine, and washing dishes and scrubbing floors and ironing shirts presents no particular intellectual challenge. She has a void to fill that the company of children will not meet. She needs adult companionship. She needs to discuss adult problems and have adult intellectual challenges. She needs to have someone on her own adult level with whom to discuss her problems, no matter how insignificant they might seem. She needs to feel like a person rather than like a machine. This is one reason, perhaps more than any other, why many married women are working.[1] They

[1] The working wife is a growing phenomenon in our society. Over 33 per cent of married women have jobs outside the home, a great many with school-age children. In this book we are concerned with this fact only as it bears on the relationship and the unity of the home. A working wife may make the development of the Christian home atmosphere more difficult. If the family motives are all materialistic ("to have more money to do the things we want"), that spirit may undermine the spiritual foundation of the home. Moving in a different circle of companions, conflicting working hours, weariness and fatigue, arrangement for child care and housework, and lack of time together might all be points of tension.

may not need the money, but they need the feeling of fulfillment, the feeling of being needed and important and wanted.
Unless husbands understand this basic need in their wives,
they are not even beginning to understand their spouses.

No matter how harried and weary he might be from his
own day and his own problems, the husband must remember
that when he enters the door of his home, he is entering
a world where lives another person, one who has moved in
her particular sphere of activity all day. He must put into
practice the Christian virtue of unselfishness and understanding in relationship to his wife. She looks forward to his coming home as a husband, not as a frustrated businessman. She
wants someone who will fulfill her needs, someone with whom
she can share her thoughts, her emotions, her experiences of
the day. She wants to be reassured that she is loved and
wanted and needed and that her husband is coming home
because she is there.

Being aware of these needs, the husband then must supply
the companionship and affection that she needs. Someone
has summarized three key considerations for the husband
always to display:

1) *Affection* — the kiss, the caress, the occasional gift, the
terms of endearment which bring warmth to the marriage
and make a woman feel he is coming home because she is
there and not because it is a convenient place to eat and
this is where his clothes are hung.

2) *Appreciation* — the marks of deference and respect,

On the other hand, the wife's working may be a result of the unity
that she feels in her home. If the husband is ill, children are to be put
through college, the husband is striving for an educational goal, and
she feels a part of his growing efforts — these might be reasons that
make the unity even more tightly knit.

We are here not interested in this problem from a sociological point
of view. From a Christian point of view, *that* a wife works is not
nearly as important as *why* she works.

the compliments that spring from the awareness of what she is contributing to the home and to the relationship.

3) *Attention* — the ability to listen and comment and respond and participate in her life with real interest.[2]

BOTH HAVE NEEDS AS PERSONS

Besides the needs that each has in his particular role in life, they have similar needs as human beings. Each needs security, affection, and a sense of achievement. Though he may not be able to verbalize it, each should be able to understand what the basic needs of his spouse are because he has them himself. And each should make it his prime concern to reach out in the fulfillment of those needs. There is no room in marriage for self-pity over the fact that the spouse does not live up to satisfying our needs. Instead of being on the receiving end, each spouse ought to concentrate on being on the giving end. More and more each thus discovers that it is in giving that he receives. Happiness can never be found. It must always be given away. But it is always in giving it away that it is found again.

SECURITY

Both husband and wife need to feel secure in each other. They must be able to trust each other implicitly under any and all circumstances. The one thing that they dare never doubt is the absolute loyalty of each other. This implies, of course, that each must prove himself worthy of that trust. Each must so conduct himself that there is no reason to question it. One can never complain that he is not trusted if he has given evidence that he is not absolutely trustworthy. Trust, like respect, can never be demanded; it must be earned. But its presence is absolutely essential. Each must have a

[2] Walter Imbiorski, *The New Cana Manual* (Delaney Publications, 206 South Grove St., Oak Park, Ill., 1957), p. 161.

place where he belongs, and where he feels he belongs, permanently and unchangeably. Each needs to feel certain that his spouse is one person with whom he can share everything, one person who will always understand him, one person who accepts him fully and completely for what he is, even in spite of what he is. This security makes for a feeling of self-confidence. Each can always feel that no matter where the other is, no matter what the other may be doing, he is undergirded with the loyalty and support of the other. If at any time one partner feels unsure of his spouse's love, if he cannot trust her unquestionably and absolutely, then his entire outlook on life will be affected, as will his work, his personality, and all his reactions. This one factor will permeate everything that he says and does.

AFFECTION

Another basic need for all people is affection. Each spouse must feel certain that he is first in the other's thoughts. This means, of course, that each must always be placing the other first in his thoughts. He must love genuinely and deeply and sincerely. Otherwise he becomes guilty of one of the greatest cruelties a man could know, that of robbing another personality of one of the things he most needs, and thus undermining his whole sense of well-being. So often husbands and wives take their loves for granted, and they do not show each other and tell each other as frequently as they ought what they mean to each other. When one wife in marital difficulties questioned her husband's love for her, he replied, "Of course I love her. I bring home the pay check every week. I work hard for her and the family. I do all I can for her. And what's more, I told her the day I married her that I loved her. What more does she want?" What she

wanted was to be reassured again and again and again. Someone has said, "A woman wants to be told that she is loved;
a man wants to be shown." The demonstration of love is
one thing that never grows old.

SENSE OF ACHIEVEMENT

Every human being needs to have the feeling of achievement and accomplishment. Everyone must feel that he is
playing an important and respectable role in life. Husbands
need that; wives need that; children need that. Through their
routines husbands and wives can quickly lose their perspectives. Their life and work can appear humdrum and boring
and insignificant. Before one can be a happy, healthy human
being, he needs to have a respect for himself and for what
he is doing. An important way for him to maintain that sense
of self-respect and accomplishment is the constant assurance
of those whom he loves. By all that they say and do, by
their glances and gestures and words, they can indicate how
they respect one another, appreciate one another, and above
all consider of vital importance the role that the other is
playing. For this reason the Christian home should be filled
with honest compliments. Too often people refrain from reminding the other what they need to hear. Many a bounteous
meal over which the wife spent many hours goes by without
an expression of appreciation. Too many a long day of many
hours spent in cleaning the house has gone by unnoticed.
Too many an additional ten dollars in the pay check has been
taken for granted by the family. Too many times we remind
each other of our mistakes, but fail to tell each other what
we need so much to hear. That we have done a good job
in this or that area is less important than that we feel we have
done a good job. And we can feel that only as we are told.

DIFFERENCES IN PERSONALITY PATTERNS

It might be well to add here also a listing of some of the common personality traits that are attributed to men and women. These will serve to point up again how each partner in marriage complements and completes the other, and how, when each understands and accepts the other for what he is, he adds immeasurably to the richness of the union. *The Cana Manual* has listed a comparison of characteristic traits. Some of these traits have been criticized, and the reader may not agree with all of the differences listed, but they do give pause for reflection.

Masculine	*Feminine*
Physically stronger	Physically weaker
More realistic	More idealistic
Logical	Intuitive
More emotionally stable	More emotionally volatile
Objective	Subjective
More factual	More fanciful
Slow judgment	Quick judgment
Literal	Tangential
Seeks love	Wants love
Self-assured	Less self-assured
Holistic thinking	Grasps details
Less adaptable	More adaptable
Less possessive	More possessive [3]

Understanding these traits thoroughly will help every couple to make a more penetrating analysis of the dynamics of their conjugal love. Husband and wife are very much alike in many ways. They are both human beings with all the needs of human beings. But they are also different from each

[3] Imbiorski, pp. 161, 162.

other. These fundamental differences show the utter folly of one partner trying to make over the other to make him fit the pattern of the other. This is impossible, and it should not be. Neither is meant to be like the other, but to understand and intertwine his life with the other. And this, in the face of the differences, presents a tremendous, but exciting challenge, bristling with adventure. It is these differences that make the home the laboratory that it is for Christian husbands and wives to live together as Christians ought to live.

CHAPTER SEVEN

Remaining a Unity

We are thinking about the intimacy, the unity, the togetherness that develops within the family circle. This unity involves, among many things, each accepting the other just as he is. It also involves a common determination to build their life within the framework of this acceptance. For a complete unity there can be no exceptions to this. Neither spouse can allow any portion of the other's background or personality to stand as a serious and lasting barrier between them. For the happiest marriage there must be a wholehearted acceptance of each other.

IN-LAWS

This unity in the Christian family relationship is so complete and so absolute that it includes much more than merely the acceptance of *each other*. It includes also the acceptance of *each other's family*. Not only do spouses marry each other, but they also take as a part of themselves everything that belongs to the other.

With marriage one "marries into the family," and his circle of relatives is expanded. If there are undesirable aspects in the family of a prospective spouse, those things should be considered before the marriage. If they are severe enough, if they cannot be accepted without reservation by the prospective marriage partner, then they may be reasons to prevent the union. But after the couple becomes married, each must realistically and maturely accept fully and without guile the circumstances that played an important role in shaping the character and personality of the other. This does not necessarily mean accepting everything that in-laws think and say and do, any more than it means accepting everything that any other person thinks and says and does. But it does mean accepting them for what they are, and above all, not holding the spouse responsible for what they are. The spouse is the product of his earlier home environment, but he is not the cause of it. He cannot be held responsible for what his relatives say and do and are.

In marriage each spouse no longer has only two parents. He has four. The parents of the one have become the parents also of the other. Each owes to the parents of his spouse the same respect, the same honor, and the same love that he owes to his own. The Fourth Commandment, "Honor thy father and thy mother" (Exodus 20:12), expands in scope for him as soon as he takes the marriage vow.

No one who is striving for real unity in his married life, and above all no Christian who is striving for such unity, can ever take the attitude of accepting the spouse but rejecting his parents. Since the parents are a part of the spouse, rejecting them would be, in a measure at least, rejecting also the spouse.

In-law relationships are an integral part of marriage. Multitudes of people express their deep appreciation for the amiable relationship that they enjoy. There are others for whom this relationship is always a source of contention. Probably for most people emotions are mixed. There are many characteristics about their "new parents" that they appreciate, and many characteristics that they dislike. This is true of our relationships with most people, not only in-laws. Human beings are so constituted that they are capable of love and of hate at the same time. And it is often true, as Duvall points out, that "it is only those we love who can hurt us most deeply. Because we love them, we expose ourselves to the pain and the problems of involvement. Strangers and those outside the family generally can do and say things that can be shrugged off with only minor annoyance, things which in the family are felt much more sharply." [1] Objectively understanding this principle will help people better understand themselves and all their relationships in the total family circle.

What is probably even more important to remember is a point that Duvall makes in this connection, namely, that "some of our mixed feelings about those who mean most to us come from within ourselves." [2] Often our failure to accept fully our in-laws is not so much because of the behavior of the in-laws as it is our reaction to their behavior. And our reaction is always an expression of our own personality lack and needs. One son- or daughter-in-law might react entirely

[1] Evelyn Duvall, *In-Laws: Pro and Con* (New York: Association Press, 1954), p. 292.

[2] Duvall, p. 293.

differently to a particular behavior pattern of an in-law than would another.

Here, for example, is a set of in-laws who in love have accepted their new son or daughter as a part of the family. They want to continue to do now for both of their children what they had heretofore been doing for only one of them. So they lavish their love by sending gifts, perhaps money, and in general wanting to be helpful. One son-in-law might be appreciative of that love. Another, who has insecurities of his own, and who does not feel absolutely certain of his worthiness and capability of being the head of his family, may resent it and may consider it interference in what are his prerogatives and rights. One cannot necessarily say that the parents are wrong. Neither can one say that the reactions of the son-in-law are wrong. The reaction of the son-in-law rather reflects his own personality weakness and makes for a tense situation.

The opposite may also be true, of course. In-laws by their indulgent attitudes may be continuing to hold on to a protective role. They satisfy their own needs by being overconcerned and overinvolved with their children. Duvall has expressed this well. "We want to be accepted. We long to belong. We desire the close, warm family ties that make us truly a big happy family. Yet, at the same time, we must feel that we are ourselves, first of all, without threat of domination, subordination, or impingement of others' ideals, values, or ways of life. This struggle in ourselves of simultaneously attaining a sense of self and a sense of belonging is reflected in our relationships within the family." [3]

The important thing for all in-laws, whether parents-in-law, children-in-law, or others-in-law to remember is that

[3] Duvall, p. 293.

in-laws, too, are people, people with their own needs and drives and desires. They are people who like every other person have their own loves and hates, their own likes and dislikes, their own needs to be wanted and accepted and needed. Generally speaking, they are not purposely or viciously trying to cause trouble or to disrupt the happiness of their relatives. They love their children or their parents, and they are concerned about their well-being. As a matter of fact, what they do seems, from their vantage point, to be the most logical and proper way to express their love and concern. It may seem different to those who are the recipients of their attentions, but that does not change the motives.

Several more things need to be understood about in-law relationships. The first is that the primary loyalty of the married couple is to the new family. Nothing, absolutely nothing, is to come between or to mar the unity of the new family circle. All compromises, all considerations, even toward relatives, must be built on that unalterable premise. Such loyalty to the new family circle means among other things that they are entitled to build their own lives, independently, according to their own pattern, without parental interference. If ever conflicts of opinion arise, or differences in values, it is the couple who works them out in their own way within the framework of their loyalty to each other.

Whereas this is inviolably true, it is never well for the couple to take its stand on a position which goes to the other extreme and says, "We will have nothing to do with our in-laws." The Fourth Commandment does not allow that. Furthermore, parents are, or at least should be, more mature and experienced. Where their experiences of life and living and more mature judgment may have valuable help to suggest, it should be listened to and accepted. Failure to take good, sound advice is never a sign of having "grown up." It is a sign of immaturity.

Above all, every spouse must remember that he views the parents of his partner from a perspective different from what he views his own. Everyone loves his own parents with a filial love. Because of this filial love he can and does overlook many of the faults in his parents. His love toward them enables him more readily to accept them as they are. He may actually not be aware of many of their shortcomings and certainly does not see fully how those shortcomings look to others, who do not have the same relationship with them that he does. On the other hand, because he does not have the same filial love toward the parents of his spouse, he can see much more objectively their faults and shortcomings. They may be shortcomings exactly the same as those in his parents, but whereas he fails to see them in his own parents, he sees them in others. The factor of filial love makes the difference.

Every Christian couple working to achieve a unity in all things understands well how the family of each now becomes also the family of the other. The problems, the personalities, and the circumstances of the families of each other become also the concern of the spouse. This kind of understanding and acceptance of each other's family is another step in achieving the goal of total marital unity.

MIXED MARRIAGES

The more one understands the completeness of the unity toward which marriage moves, the more one can begin to appreciate some of the difficulties involved in mixed marriages. By mixed marriage we mean not only two people who happen to belong to two different denominations. It goes much deeper than this. It is true, of course, that when a Roman Catholic and a Protestant, or a Jew and a Protestant, marry, then there is a mixed marriage. But it is also true that two Roman Catholics or two Lutherans or two Presbyterians may be involved in a mixed marriage.

Religion involves a great deal more than merely maintaining membership in the same church. The word "religion" is derived from the Latin word "religere" and means "to tie together." One's religion is that which ties him together, that which makes him what he is, that which makes him think what he thinks, believe what he believes, and go after what he goes after. His religion is that which determines his sense of values and makes him the kind of person that he is. It determines his hopes and his dreams, his likes and his dislikes, the things he holds dear and the things he shuns. Religion is not merely a façade to the building of life. It is the foundation. Every person, even the atheist, has a religion. The question never is whether a person is religious, but rather what his religion is.

It is very possible for two people belonging to the same church to be poles apart in their religious thinking and in their basic views. One may be a sincere and dedicated Christian. All his motivations, his hopes, his goals for time and eternity center in Christ and are motivated by his relationship to Christ. The other may be a nominal Christian only, a member of the church because of habit or expediency, but one who remains unmoved, unchanged, untouched by the good news of Christianity. To one the discipline and exercise of his Christianity may be meaningful, to the other it may be merely peripheral. For one, every goal in life may be determined by his Christian principles; for the other, goals may be built upon materialistic and humanistic values. Such people will not think alike, and their marriage is mixed, regardless of their denominational affiliation.

A young man once approached John Wesley to seek his advice regarding his forthcoming marriage. After some thought Wesley replied that he did not think that this was the girl for the young man. The young man, who obviously had come more for encouragement than for advice, replied, "Why not, she's a Christian, isn't she?" And then Wesley replied, "Yes, but there are some Christians with whom only God can live." People should not delude themselves into thinking that simply because they are members of the same church that therefore they have the same religion.

When one chooses a partner for life, he should want someone who thinks as he does on the fundamental and basic questions of life, one who is pushing toward the same goals, who has the same basic philosophy and outlook toward life in general and marriage in particular. It is this that provides the solid foundation upon which the couple may build their home. It is this that establishes the base on which they can resolve the other differences that they encounter in each other. Without this unity in the basic things they have less common ground on which they can begin to build their lives firmly together.

Religion is the cementing tie. When, for example, both have the same concept of the importance of prayer or the worthwhileness of family worship, or when both believe firmly in divine forgiveness and divine providence, then they have a common starting point from which to begin to build. When both are concerned genuinely about developing a Christian atmosphere in their home, then there are two people working together toward a common goal. Different though they may be as individuals, their common goal serves to unite them.

Religion, real heart religion, manifests itself again and again in everyday attitudes that spouses manifest toward each other, and certainly also in many experiences of their life together.

Here, for exmple, is a family whose child is ill. The doctor doesn't know what the outcome will be. What could bring the two parents together more closely and more meaningfully than their sincere and genuine trust in the goodness of God that drives them to bring their need and concern together before the Throne of Grace? When a couple has had difficulty in a personality adjustment, what could tie them together more closely than each of them looking the other in the eye and praying together the Fifth Petition of the Lord's Prayer, "Forgive us our trespasses as we forgive those who trespass against us" — as we forgive each other.

When the religion in a home is mixed, there is not a complete thinking together, a complete oneness in the things that are basically and fundamentally important. There are those who think they have found the solution to the problem by making religion one matter that they do not discuss in their family. What they fail to see is that religion is much more than merely an "organized" discipline. Whether it is discussed or not, the religious factor will always be present. What is more, the solution to any problem never lies in refraining from or refusing to discuss it. That only serves to dam up honest feelings. The very fact that there is one thing, no matter how small, that stands between husband and wife, one thing that cannot be discussed openly and freely and frankly, one thing that cannot be talked out, indicates immediately that there is at least one barrier between them, one hindrance to a relationship of complete and mutual sharing of everything that they are. The ideal marriage is one where *both* husband and wife see "eye to eye" in their religious thinking and where each attempts to live according to the precepts of his Christianity. It is this that makes the marriage specifically Christian.

All marriage studies indicate that a similarity of religious background makes for greater chances of success in marriage.[4]

The converse is also true. Where there is dissimilarity in religious values, additional tensions and problems arise that need solution. The difficulties that arise have often been enumerated. John Wynn makes the statement: "It is estimated that more than half of the men in mixed marriages and more than a third of the women drop their church contacts altogether."[5] And David Mace lists five areas of tension that are bound to occur in every mixed marriage and which must be faced:

1. Differences in religious attitudes are fundamental differences.

2. Religious differences always imply wide areas of conflict.

3. Church loyalties and family loyalties will usually clash.

4. Tensions with in-laws are often acute.

5. The upbringing of children presents constant problems.[6]

The convention of The Lutheran Church — Missouri Synod in 1959 adopted a statement on Interfaith or Mixed Marriages. Regarding the general principles involved it said, in part:

[4] Evelyn Duvall and Reuben Hill, *When You Marry* (New York: Association Press, 1953), p. 390.

[5] John Wynn, *Pastoral Ministry to Families* (Philadelphia: Westminster Press, 1957), p. 118.

[6] David Mace, "The Truth About Mixed Marriages," *Woman's Home Companion* (July 1951), p. 44.

In marriage, as in personal life, spiritual factors are of primary concern. For Christians, the highest expression of mutual love in marriage is comparable to the redeeming love of Christ of His church (Ephesians 5:18-33; Revelation 21:2-9). Something less than this high ideal may obtain in a marriage because of variant factors which may in turn disturb or endanger its well-being and be detrimental to family relationships and to the training of the children. Factors which militate against or obviate the spiritual unity of the marriage are of special concern to the church in its ministry to families. *Differences in religious beliefs and attitudes are fundamental differences which imply wide areas of conflict in church and family loyalties, responsibilities, and relationships.*[7]

Those who have embarked on a mixed marriage need not be reminded of these tensions. They will recognize immediately that a mixed marriage means that there are problem areas that need to be solved. The type of conflict will vary, depending not only upon the personalities of the people involved, but also upon the nature of the mixed marriage. Each presents its own peculiar difficulties. One principle, however, is true through them all. Marriage is inviolate, and husbands and wives must apply every principle of love to work out difficulties that arise from them.[8]

[7] *Proceedings* of the Forty-fourth Regular Convention of The Lutheran Church — Missouri Synod, San Francisco, Calif., 1959, p. 207.

[8] This book does not pretend to discuss the specific problems of marriages. Others do that. This book is meant to show Christian couples the beauty of *unity* in marriage. If you need further help in the area of mixed marriage, the specific problems of mixed marriages are fully covered in such helps as the following, listed in the bibliography:

Statement on Interfaith Marriages, Lutheran Church — Missouri Synod, Board of Parish Education, 1959

James Pike, *If You Marry Outside Your Faith*

Bossard and Boll, *One Marriage — Two Faiths*

Bossard and Letts, *Mixed Marriage Involving Lutherans*

National Council of Churches, *If I Marry a Roman Catholic*, 23 pages

Divorce

From everything that has been said about the unity of
marriage we can understand why the Bible takes such a dim
view of divorce. If in marriage two people have become
united into a oneness, a unity, then a divorce is tearing apart
something that is essentially one. It is like cutting up a body,
like taking that which is one and sawing it in half. Divorce
is mutilation.

From the Christian point of view, only He who established
and instituted marriage has the right to break it up. That
is a prerogative that belongs to God alone. He will one day
in His own wisdom separate the Christian spouses from each
other in death. Whenever human beings assume for themselves a right which is a prerogative of God, they are assuming for themselves rights and privileges that are divine. The
fact that divorce carries less social stigma than it once did,
and that it is more commonly accepted than it once was,
does not alter the principle. The Christian's behavior is
determined not by human standards but by divine precepts.

There are times when individuals are justified in breaking up their marriage. Scripture itself allows for the fact
that fornication is justification for "putting away one's wife"
(Matthew 19:9). But whenever fornication (breaking the
vow of faithfulness to each other) occurs, then the unfaithful partner has become guilty of adulterating the marriage,
of trampling upon its sanctity. He has already by that act
broken the unit relationship with his partner. He has entered
into a "one flesh" relationship with another. The divorce
then is merely the public proclamation of that fact.

However, when fornication has occurred, this does not
make it the duty of the Christian spouse to put away his
unfaithful partner. Christ *permits,* but does not *command,*

married people to divorce if one has become guilty of fornication (Matthew 5:31, 32; 19:9). Reconciliation is always the goal toward which all Christians strive. Paul says: "To the married I give charge, not I but the Lord, that the wife should not separate from her husband (but if she does, let her remain single or else be reconciled to her husband) — and that the husband should not divorce his wife" (1 Corinthians 7:11 RSV). If at all possible, the unfaithful partner should be brought to a penitent attitude toward his or her immoral conduct, and the faithful partner should manifest all the love and forgiveness that a Christian knows. With penitence on the one hand and forgiveness on the other, trust and confidence might again be built up and the unity restored. One of the most difficult things for a partner to forget and overcome in marriage is such unfaithfulness. The hurt is difficult to suppress. But this is a test of the greatness of his love.

Continued and willful unfaithfulness on the part of one or the other spouse, however, poses another problem. It is an obvious flaunting of what God meant marriage to be, and such a person is a "deserter" and shows himself unfit and unworthy to be a Christian spouse.

The Bible also indicates that if an unbelieving, that is, non-Christian, partner in marriage "departs" and becomes guilty of desertion, then there is nothing that the Christian can do about it (1 Corinthians 7:15). It must be noted though that it is always the non-Christian (the "unbelieving," 1 Corinthians 7:15), not the Christian, who becomes the deserter. No Christian could ever think of leaving his family. Marriage to him is always a sacred union. The person who is really a Christian, who thinks and lives as a Christian, has also a Christian concept of the permanence of marriage.

One thing is always true. Whenever a divorce occurs, this is contrary to the divine ordinance which says, "What God hath joined together, let not man put asunder" (Matthew 19:6). It is always, without exception, the result of one or both partners not living and acting as Christians should live and act. Marriage, under God's ordinance, is for keeps! When divorce happens, this does not *change* the rule. It *violates* the rule.

Whereas this Biblical principle is unquestionably clear, the problem of possible divorce rises in many homes — and for reasons other than the Scripturally sanctioned reasons. Marriage involves physical, social, emotional, psychological, financial, and spiritual factors. Differences will arise in some or even all of these areas constantly, sometimes to the point where they seem beyond repair. When they do occur, the marriage is sick. The severity of its illness depends upon the depth of the maladjustment in any one area or upon the number of areas in which adjustments have not been properly made. Whenever there is physical illness, however, one does not solve the problem by destroying himself. He goes rather to a physician to have his illness diagnosed and to seek a cure. The measures taken then depend upon the nature and severity of the illness. So in marriage. When something is wrong, the first solution should not be one of destroying the marriage, but rather one of seeking a diagnosis and soliciting help in healing the breaches. The Christian never loses sight of the fact that his marriage, even in its unhappier moments, is sacred.

But the Christian, too, is concerned with more than holding his marriage together simply for the sake of holding it together, or for the sake of the children, or for the sake of the relatives, or for the sake of reputation. In a Christian marriage both partners are concerned about building the unity of their marriage, and about reacting to all their problems, some of which may call for help, *as Christians,* within the context of marital permanence. Because of this, forgiveness and reconciliation are daily features in every Christian home. Christians are daily living by the precepts that Paul enunciates so often, so clearly, and so specifically. "Put on then, as God's chosen ones, holy and beloved, compassion, kindness, lowliness, meekness, and patience, forbearing one another and, if one has a complaint against another, forgiving each other; as the Lord has forgiven you, so you must also forgive. And above all these put on love, which binds everything together in perfect harmony. . . . Wives, be subject to your husbands, as is fitting in the Lord. Husbands, love your wives, and do not be harsh with them." (Colossians 3:12-14, 18, 19 RSV)

When husbands and wives live by these principles, divorce is unthinkable. And husbands and wives, both of them, will live by these principles — if they are living as Christians.

CHAPTER EIGHT

Physical Unity

We have in the preceding chapters been talking only about the first purpose of marriage, namely, that of companionship (see page 32). We have been pointing to the growing unity that develops between husband and wife spiritually, economically, socially, intellectually. This relationship of unity in love continues to develop in the day-by-day companionship that each finds in the other. Now this unity that is developing finds expression in still another way, in physical union, in the total giving of their physical selves to each other. The physical intimacy of marriage, in which each unreservedly and unashamedly submits his total physical self to the other, serves a twofold purpose. On the one hand, it is an expression of the unity that exists in the marriage, and on the other hand, it becomes a *unifying factor* in the marriage, making the total union that much more beautiful. The sex relationship is one of many interacting relationships in which the couple constantly finds itself. This is all intended in Genesis, where the principle is given that "a man shall leave his father and his mother and shall cleave unto his wife, and they shall be one flesh." (Genesis 2:24)

Whenever Scripture uses the term "one flesh," it always has in mind the total oneness of married partners and includes the physical, sexual relationship between husband and wife. The unity of companionship is climaxed by the union of bodies, thus making the unity complete.

Sex Is More Than a Biological Function

The sex function is a great deal more than merely the satisfaction of physical and biological urges. With animals it is no more than that. It is merely a part of the process of procreation. Since animals are not morally responsible creatures and since the sex function is merely the biological provision for progeny, promiscuity is the rule. But human beings have reason and intelligence. They plan and form judgments. They control and discipline themselves. They are moral beings, accountable and responsible for their actions. For them the sex act, as all other behavior, has within it moral implications. Its function goes beyond that of begetting children. It is a symbol and expression of the unity existing between husband and wife. It is performed by two people whose personalities have dignity. It involves the wishes and desires of several people.

Sex Has Moral Implications

There are spiritual overtones to everything that Christians do. "Whether therefore ye eat or drink or whatsoever ye do, do all to the glory of God" (1 Corinthians 10:31). "Whatsoever ye do in word or deed, do all in the name of the Lord Jesus" (Colossians 3:17). In the Christian's philosophy of life, motivation becomes very important. He does everything "in the name of the Lord Jesus" and "to the glory of God."

Eating is good; but it may also be wrong under certain circumstances. If one overeats, or eats what he should not eat for reasons of health, then he is harming his body. Physical exercise is necessary, but it may become wrong under certain circumstances. If a person constantly engages in exercise so violent that it is harmful to health, or exercises when he has been committed to absolute rest, it is wrong.

Because of his commitment to Christ the Christian strives always to bring "into captivity every thought to the obedience of Christ" (2 Corinthians 10:5). He learns to control his drives and his needs and thus becomes a mature and disciplined personality. To the extent that he does not control his behavior he becomes an immature and undisciplined personality, self-centered and selfish.

It is not different with the sex drive. It also, together with all other aspects of the Christian's life, needs to be controlled and disciplined. The Christian controls his sex impulses as he controls his hunger and thirst drives. He knows that there is a proper and an improper use of all God-given functions.

If the sex act carries with it moral overtones, then also in marriage it has moral implications. Husbands and wives have complete sexual freedom with each other, but this freedom is always exercised within the framework of Christian thinking. Christian love permeates also romantic love. And love always means a profound understanding of and concern for the person loved. This applies with double force in the matter of sexual relationships, where understanding and love are so necessary to make them mutually satisfactory.

DIFFERENCES IN THE SEX ROLE

It has been a part of God's ordinance that men and women have been made different from one another, also so far as the sex role is concerned. Also in the sexual area of life man ordinarily is the aggressor, the leader, while the woman is the recipient of his love. This, however, is not a rigid rule, because sex play is love play, and there must be a mutual manifestation of love. Neither of the partners can be passive and still achieve from the sexual relationships the highest degree of satisfaction. Real love, after all, is concerned about giving. This holds true for wives as well as for husbands. For the male, however, sex drives are ordinarily more easily aroused. For him the sexual act provides a strong biological satisfaction and release of tension. This may be true of the woman, too, and often is. Her responses, however, are usually not as quick as those of her husband. Psychologically and physiologically she is so constituted that the sex act represents to her more of a total giving of herself to her husband. Her enjoyment comes as much from the symbolism of her total belonging to her husband, and his wanting her completely, as from the physical climax itself.

The husband must recognize the differences between himself and his wife, that her responses are slower, that her needs are less easily aroused, and that it is her total set of mind and feeling that determines whether she is ready for physical union. The husband might feel, for example, that physical relationships are the normal climax to settling of differences that they have had during the day, but the wife, because of the differences, is not yet in a state of emotional readiness for such relationship.

The wife, on the other hand, must understand that her husband's physical make-up is such that biologically he needs sexual relationships as a release of tension. He is attracted to her and she is attractive to him. He therefore sees her physical beauty and thinks of their relationships as an expression of his love to her. The woman understands that when her husband wants her physically, it is not because he thinks of her as a "plaything," but because she is wholly attractive to him. Instead of complaining about this, she should consider it a high compliment. And basically, as she thinks the matter through, she wants to be wanted by her husband, and she wants to appeal to him.

Each then tries to understand the other: the husband being patient with his wife's slowness of response and sometimes even lack of desire for physical relationships, and the wife being aware of his more immediate need. Never should the sex act be a matter of one partner merely "giving in" to the other. Always it should be a matter of each "giving over" to the other. This is an expression of their unity in marriage.

PHYSICAL ASPECTS OF SEX

There are many physical aspects of the sex relationship that could be discussed: the frequency of intercourse, the intensity of foreplay, and various positions possible for the sex act itself; but these physical aspects of the relationships are not within the intent of this book. Many books have been written on this subject. The bibliography at the end of this book will suggest some. When husbands and wives love each other with the intensity of love that they should have, when each is concerned always with pleasing the other, then many of the physical aspects and problems of the sexual relationships take care of themselves. One cannot learn understanding and patience and love from reading a book. It must be practiced.

This, however, can be said unequivocally: the Christian concept of marital love must and does include *eros*. Husbands and wives know no limits in their efforts to please each other sexually. They will constantly seek out new methods and means by which they can afford satisfaction to each other.

Sex and Marital Problems

Whenever couples have problems in their marital adjustments, these problems often show themselves in the sexual relationships. This is the area that is usually affected by such problems, because this is the area where husband and wife are most intimate and which, since it is literally a love act, is the first to be touched when love is not as evident as it ought to be. Very frequently husbands will complain that their wives are frigid and do not understand their needs, and wives will retaliate that the only reason that their husbands married them was for sex. Couples should always remember that when they are having problems in the area of their sex lives, these problems are seldom the cause of their difficulties and differences, but merely symptoms of them. Whenever adjustments are not made in the area of sex, it is usually an indication that satisfactory adjustments were not made in the companionship area of their marriage. A unity has not been achieved there. Since they have not come to feel a oneness, they have no oneness to express to each other in the intimacy of the marital bed. Hence whenever couples are having problems in the area of sex, they need to look deeper into their relationship with each other and to mend their fences and improve their growing unity in their day-by-day experiences with each other.

PURPOSE OF SEX

There are some who feel that the only or the prime purpose of sex is the procreation of children. This is not true. Sex has a place by itself and in its own right. One of the God-given purposes of sex is that it is the climax of the "one flesh" relationship that exists between husband and wife. It is a function in which each gives himself fully to the other and finds joy and happiness in so doing. The Bible often uses the expression "to know" when it speaks of physical relationships. "And Adam knew Eve, his wife" (Genesis 4:1). This is more than a polite way of stating a rather personal fact. It is literally true that in physical relationships husbands and wives do get to know each other fully. They know each other in one of the most intimate ways possible. They learn to know each other's needs and drives and feelings, as well as the other's inhibitions and fears. They come to understand the deeper motivations of their partner. Never does one get to know the real person as much as when his emotions are at a high pitch. That is when one can tell whether a person is basically self-centered or outgoing in his love, whether he is basically patient and understanding or whether he is basically demanding and thoughtless. In the sex act, with all barriers down, husbands and wives undergo a significant experience in learning to know each other just as they are.

That sex has a place in its own right in marriage is made clear to us in the New Testament. Paul reminds husbands and wives: "The husband should give to his wife her conjugal rights, and likewise the wife to her husband. For the wife does not rule over her own body, but the husband does; likewise the husband does not rule over his own body, but the wife does. Do not refuse one another except perhaps by agreement for a season, that you may devote yourselves to prayer; but then come together again, lest Satan tempt you through lack of self-control" (1 Corinthians 7:3-5 RSV). In this passage Paul is telling us several things.

For one thing, he is reminding us of the fact that physical relationships are a part of conjugal rights and privileges, and to refuse them to each other is to deny each other what rightfully belongs to the other.

He is stressing, too, what we have been stressing so frequently in these pages, namely, that marriage is not made up of two individuals, but has become one unit. He states very clearly that the wife does "not have power over her own body, but the husband does," and also that the husband "does not have power over his own body, but the wife does." In other words, the body of each belongs to the other, not to himself. Here we have the ultimate and supreme meaning of Paul's expression, alluded to earlier, that one's spouse is one's "other self" (Ephesians 5:28). This is a tremendously beautiful and significant concept. Each feels completely, entirely, totally a part of the other, and hence each gives himself completely, entirely, totally to the other.

One pastor tells this somewhat amusing incident. He had been lecturing on this thought at a summer camp. That afternoon two men were playfully scuffling in the sand on the beach, when the one said to the other, "You leave your hands off my wife's body." The statement was meant to be facetious. But it does have behind it a deeper truth. The husband's body is really that of his wife; the wife's body is that of her husband. Wonderfully, totally, completely so!

Because this is true, these bodies now become "private property." Each is rigidly adamant about a "hands off" policy. For anyone else to trespass on the sacred possession of our spouse is trampling on holy ground. No husband or wife should even think of letting another person violate this sacred trust by laying hands on or allowing hands to be laid on that which does not belong to them. They have given their bodies to their spouses in marriage. Any person who does not observe this is violating the property rights of others.

Sex Is Holy

When husband and wife give themselves to each other fully in marriage, then sex is beautiful. It has a high and holy and giving purpose. It is an expression of the unity of the married estate. Outside of marriage, however, sexual relations are always lustful. There it is always selfish. Extramarital relationships, unfaithfulness on the part of husband or wife, is always not only cheating, but it is also the direct result of one's wanting his own wishes and desires satisfied, even at the cost of moral aberration. It is a matter of being willing to throw over God's will for the sake of his own. Thus this sin of fornication has at its base the sin of selfishness, placing ourselves ahead of God. This can never be in the life of people who are striving to "love the Lord, their God, with all their heart and with all their soul and with all their mind." (Matthew 22:37)

The same principle holds true for premarital sexual relationships. These are the unwarranted, immediate satisfying of strong sexual impulses, the result of a lack of self-control and self-discipline. The thing that makes sex proper and beautiful and Christian is the total setting into which sex relationships fit. Sex in marriage is not an end in itself, as it so often is in premarital relationships. It is a part of the total marital picture. If the marital aspects are torn away, nothing is left but the selfish husks.

Sex, then, in its proper place is good. It is a part of God's creation. It is meant for the mutual enjoyment of husband and wife. It is the failure to understand this that has caused some people to be confused in their logic when thinking through the matter of birth control or planned parenthood.

FEARS OF SEX

Sometimes people, probably most often women, bring to their marriage many taboos, fears, complexes regarding sex, so much so at times that they find it difficult to make adequate adjustments. Many times they must eliminate these taboos before they can feel a complete and uninhibited freedom in their marital expression. They must learn to understand themselves and their fears and unwarranted inhibitions before they can eliminate them.

On the other hand though, partners must always reach out in understanding each other, or as the Scripture says, in "knowing each other." The situation calls for an extra amount of patience and understanding, kindness and love, on the part of the husband in order that he might help his fearful wife overcome some of her inhibitions and help her grow and develop, so that she might lose all her compunctions and become everything that she should be as a totally committed wife. On her part it means a growing understanding of the beauty and sacredness of the physical relationship as an expression of her love to her husband. In either case, love must reign supreme.

CHAPTER NINE

The Crowning Unity

In the Christian concept of marriage, children play a very beautiful role. Husband and wife have been spending much time and many efforts in growing together into a unity, emotionally, intellectually, spiritually, economically. They have climaxed this growing unity with a physical unity in their sexual relationships. And now God permits this couple, which has grown and is continuing to grow together into a oneness, to do something together that neither of them could do separately. He permits them to have a child. He allows them to have a share in the creation of another life. In a sense the child represents the climax of the unity of the marriage, because the child is truly a part of both of its parents, and both of the parents have a part in the child. It is a product of the companionship and love and unity that husband and wife have shown toward each other and will forever stand as that symbol. It is God's crowning blessing upon the unity that husband and wife have achieved. And all of the unity that has been developed between husband and wife will now be employed for the benefit of the new life which their unity produced.

CHILDREN AS GIFTS FROM GOD

Children, from the Christian point of view, are never merely biological accidents. They are not simply the natural results of married life. They certainly are not the "punishment" that one must bear for the privilege of marital relationships. Children are in a very real sense "bundles from heaven." No laboratory can create human life; no individual can create human life; and no set of parents, regardless of how many children they have, can create life. The miracle of the procreative process is something that only God can perform. Whenever a mother's ovum is fertilized by a sperm and after some months she delivers a fully developed child, one of the most stupendous miracles in all of nature has taken place.

Christian couples understand that. They therefore regard their children as unique blessings and trusts from God. In one sense they see their offspring not as "their children" but as "God's children." They view their relationship with their children as that of "baby sitters for God." They understand that they are caretakers for God of a sacred and precious heritage and that they therefore have an important stewardship responsibility. They could think of nothing less than of doing their best in the matter of loving, rearing, helping, and guiding these treasures that God has placed into their care.

This attitude toward children makes a tremendous difference in the way parents will handle and rear them. If instead of thinking of their child as a gift of God, either or both parents did not want the child, or resented the pregnancy, or thought of the child as a frustration of their freedoms or as a burden and responsibility, then those parents' attitudes are going to reflect in their attitudes toward their children. They certainly are not going to be able to share with the child all of the love and understanding to which the child as an individual is entitled and which it so much needs. Parents' attitudes toward their children will have much more to do with shaping the child's own attitudes toward itself and life than all the things that the parent does for the child in a material way.

WHEN CHILDREN ARE ADOPTED

There are times when God withholds from couples the privilege of having children of their own. In many cases they will adopt one. When they do this, everything that applies to a child born into the union by natural processes applies also to a child brought into the union by legal processes. The mere fact that the parents want to bring another life into their family circle is already evidence that they have a unity to share. Christian parents do not accord such a child the same treatment *as if* it were their own. It *is* their own — just as really and integrally as if they themselves had conceived it and given birth to it. It is a gift of God to them. For them the fact that the child is adopted is only a legal technicality. Not a single parental joy or responsibility is withheld from them.

CHILDREN AND HOME STABILITY

It has been said that children make the home. This may be true. Children often do help in establishing a family unity that was not present before, because they now represent a common interest and a common concern on the part of the parents. Their presence may help the parents mature and make what for each of them up to this time had been "inner-directed" thoughts "other-directed." In focusing our concerns to another object we often forget ourselves and begin to learn the meaning of gracious self-sacrifice and self-denial.

This, however, is not always the case. Sometimes the self-centeredness and immaturity of parents is so great that not even the needs of a child are strong enough to draw them into a unity, and the child becomes a source of contention and serves to widen the gulf that already exists between husband and wife. Instead of drawing them closer together, their differing attitudes in the problems of child rearing might only be emphasized. If this happens, parents need to understand that it is not their problems concerning their children that caused their differences, but rather their differences that showed up in the rearing of their children. They need, for their own sakes and for the sake of the children whom they are rearing, to look carefully to how they are adjusting to each other.

In a Christian home, however, it is taken for granted that from the very beginning of the marriage the parents are on their way to a unity. The children now come and are regarded as a climaxing result of the unity that has already been established. Christian parents look to their children, not as a means whereby they might develop their unity, but as objects with whom they might share their unity and express it further. When Christian parents have grown together in their companionship, when they have become compatible in expressing their love to each other in a physical way, then the togetherness that they have is something they can apply to the rearing of their children.

CHILDREN AND PARENTHOOD

Realizing that their children are gifts and blessings of God, parents will look forward to this blessing in their home. They recognize that their children provide them the opportunity to share with a future generation the unity they have acquired. This is important. Parents sometimes think that the success of their parenthood is dependent upon what they can provide for their children in a material way in food, clothing, education, and advantages. Their standards sometimes become more a reflection of their own feelings of lack and inadequacy than what is actually good for the child. What they want to provide for their children is often what they feel they missed in their own childhood. They compare their own parenthood with that of their own parents. What they feel their parents lacked, they now try to provide, and they may succeed. What they fail to see is that while they are providing for their own children what their parents did not provide for them, they are at the same time not providing other things for their own children. These in turn will grow up with certain lacks and will again reflect the feeling of those lacks upon their own children. Thus each generation of parents continues, feeling that something was lacking in their childhood homes, trying to compensate for it in the ones they establish, but omitting something else.

Parents also sometimes read their own desires and dreams into the lives of their children. What they feel they missed they want their children to become. Perhaps they badly wanted a college education and at all costs then drive a child, even though he may not be of college caliber, to that end. Perhaps they dreamed of a life in music or athletics or a profession. Always they must take care lest what they think is their child's needs is not really a reflection of their own. Each child is an individual with his own particular and individual capabilities, and that child's needs are determined by its own individual personality.

THE NEEDS OF CHILDREN

There are some basic needs that every child, like every adult, has. When we can supply these psychological needs, we have provided him with more riches than if we made him the recipient of every material blessing in the world.

SECURITY

The first of these is security. He needs to be free from anxiety and fear. He needs to feel safe and confident and not be afraid of people and things. Inadvertently, by remarks, by their own fears, and more often by their own efforts at discipline, parents instill in their children fears of certain situations or people.

The child must, moreover, feel that he fits and that he is genuinely wanted in the family circle. This security is something that no amount of talking will establish; it must be communicated to him by the parents.

Insecure parents will, no matter how hard they may try not to, leave insecurities also with their children. They cannot give to their children what they themselves do not first have. If, for example, the wife is uncertain about her husband, is never quite sure whether he will be home for dinner, always feels that his behavior is unpredictable, never knows when he is going to throw a temper tantrum; or if the husband is constantly wondering whether he is genuinely loved by his wife or merely tolerated as a necessary evil, or if he is made to feel that his pay check is more important than he is, or if he is not absolutely certain of his wife's respect and loyalty, then those uncertainties will be caught by the child. They will be part of the atmosphere which it breathes.

All characteristics of the parents will have an effect upon

the child from the moment it is born. Their own nervousness and tension, their own pettiness and insecurity will react on the child. So will their mutual love and unity, understanding and thoughtfulness. Parents who have developed these positive Christian attitudes in their own relationship with each other will unconsciously be sharing them with their offspring. A part of what we are always rubs off on the people with whom we associate, and most certainly upon those who depend upon us to see what life should be like.

AFFECTION

The child also needs affection. More than anything else it needs to be loved and to feel that it is loved. Sometimes we hold the mistaken notion that we show our love by the material things that we do for the child, the gifts we give, the clothes we provide. Love is shown, however, not so much by what we do *for* the child as by what we do *to* it. Oftentimes a lavish abundance of material advantages made available for the child are in reality compensations on the part of the parents to make up for hidden feelings of not doing to the child all that they ought, of not giving of their own selves to the child. No amount of material advantages will take the place of the total loving involvement of the parent himself in the child's life.

Like all Christian love, the love of the parent for the child is entirely outgoing, concerned with the feelings and welfare of the child. Many parents who love their child and who discipline their child and who are concerned about doing "what is good for the child" are in reality not loving the child as much as they are loving themselves. Their discipline of the child is more the spur-of-the-moment type of discipline. It is a discipline inflicted because what the child does displeases them at the moment, or occurs when they are in a bad mood, rather than because the child needs discipline for the formation of its character. Discipline which is emotionally fraught will always be inconsistent. Real Christian love, real helpfulness to the child shows itself always by thinking of the *child* first. When, for example, the child has rebelled, the parent may react strongly by insisting that "the child flouted my authority and needs a lesson." This is a parent-centered reaction. Or the parent may react by saying, "The child is trying to discover its own sense of importance." That is a child-centered reaction (love is always other-centered) and evokes an altogether different attitude and type of discipline on the child.

It ought to be self-understood that the child has the affection and love of both parents. Each parent plays a different role in the home and also in the eyes of the child. But the child must always feel that no matter what happens to it, no matter what mistakes it makes, it is still loved and appreciated and understood by its parents.

It happens in the life of all parents that they look back to see mistakes they have made in the rearing of their children. They wonder whether they have been too firm or too lenient, whether they have been too rigid or too lax, whether they have made too many rules or not enough, whether they have permitted their children to do too much or whether they said "no" too often, whether they have given them too much for their own good or whether perhaps they haven't done enough for them. Conscientious parents will always be engaged in self-examination. Generally though, parents may take this consolation: if they genuinely love their children and if all of their training of their children takes place within the framework of real love and affection, they need not be concerned. They may have made many mistakes, but these mistakes, taking place within the framework of love, will not seriously damage the child.

UNDERSTANDING

The third need of the child is understanding. Every child, like every adult, is an individual. He has his strong points and he has his weak points. He is different from every other child in the world, including his brothers and sisters, in looks, in personality, in intelligence, in aptitudes, and in emotional response. And he as an individual has a right to be himself just as every adult has that right. He has a right, too, to expect not to be compared with his brothers and sisters or friends.

He will not always react to situations as his parents would like to see him react. First of all, he is not as mature as they. Parents react to situations from their adult point of view, which is, or ought to be, much more mature than that of the child. Then, too, he is a personality entirely different from his parents. He needs to be understood and accepted for what he is.

SENSE OF ACHIEVEMENT

And finally, the child needs a sense of achievement. He must realize his worth and value as a person. He must feel a sense of dignity toward himself before he can show respect to others. He needs the sense of contributing to, and being a part of, the family circle and, above all, of being appreciated for what he is contributing. There is nothing more discouraging to any individual (thus to a child too) than the feeling that what he is and what he is trying to do goes unnoticed and unappreciated. Nothing can more quickly cause anyone to stop attempting to please. This happens so often when parents do not praise and show appreciation enough for little accomplishments. They are quick to criticize, feeling that they are helping the child by correcting its mistakes. But always "helping" by showing a person where he is wrong and seldom encouraging him when he is right is one of the most crushing experiences that can happen to an individual. Think how we coddle and encourage a child when we are teaching it to walk. We know that it is encouragement and not scolding that produces results. (We recognize this psychology even with our dogs.) All during childhood and adulthood, too, everyone needs something of this kind of encouragement to give him a sense of achievement.

These needs can be satisfied in a child only by the cooperative efforts of both parents. Neither one of them can do it alone. If they do not both see together in this matter and work together lovingly, then the only result can be confusion and frustration in the child. This is especially true if there are open conflicts and antagonisms and misunderstandings on the part of the parents. The rearing of children is a job for a team, for the unit of husband wife to accomplish together.[1]

[1] Louis Burke, *With This Ring* (New York: McGraw-Hill Book Company, Inc., 1958), pp. 270—280. — As Judge of the Superior Court of Los Angeles County, Judge Burke saw and heard thousands of marriage difficulties. He became convinced that in many instances difficulties occurred because the married people did not know what was expected of them. He conceived the idea of putting the hopes and promises of each partner of the marriage into writing and to let "each party sign the statement as a binding document for future action." The Agreement contains the following sections: Marital Counseling; Forgetting the Past; Division of Responsibility in the Home; Support of the Family; Welfare of the Children; Husband's Role in the Family; Falling Out of Love; A Normal Married Life; Privacy; Mutual Friends; Alcoholic Beverages; Speaking in a Normal Tone of Voice; Sarcastic, Belittling Remarks; Silent Treatment; Religion; Love and Affection; Consideration for the

ONE-PARENT FAMILIES

When we say that the rearing of children is a job for a team, that implies, of course, that there are two parents in the home. There can hardly be such a "team" relationship in a one-parent home. In such instances the problem of parental tension or lack of co-operation on the part of one is never present. The problem then is a different one. The remaining parent must in a sense assume greater responsibilities, attempting to be both father and mother to the child. This has been achieved valiantly and nobly by many individuals. That their task is more difficult will be attested to by everyone in such a situation, but that it can be accomplished effectively and successfully is also a fact, as seen from the lives of many well-adjusted children from one-parent homes.

WHAT CHILDREN EXPECT

We speak often as adults to adults what we should be doing for our children. Sometimes we forget that children might tell us better than we can what their needs and wants are.

A few years ago Dr. F. R. Hertz, a British author and psychologist, asked 100,000 children between the ages of 8 and 14 from all walks of life in 24 countries to make a list of ten rules of behavior for parents. This is the list of what the majority of the children voted for:

1. Do not quarrel in front of your children.

Other Person's Feelings; Recognition of Accomplishments; Nagging; Mealtimes; Tolerance of Friends and Relatives; Social Activities; Late Hours; Third Persons in the Home; Children; Sexual Intercourse; The Importance of Lovemaking; Household Expenses; Pocket Money; Charge Accounts; An End to the Day's Problems; Family Prayer. — The section on children is quoted in Appendix I to this book.

2. Treat all your children with equal affection.

3. Never lie to a child.

4. There must be mutual tolerance between parents.

5. There should be comradeship between parents and children.

6. Treat your children's friends as welcome visitors in the home.

7. Always answer children's questions.

8. Don't blame or punish your child in the presence of children from next door.

9. Concentrate on your child's good points. Do not over-emphasize his failings.

10. Be constant in your affection and mood.[2]

WHAT PARENTS ARE IS MORE IMPORTANT THAN WHAT THEY SAY

From all this it is clear that the child's development is determined more by what its parents *are* than by what they *say*. The child is born into a unit, and a part of what that unit is rubs off on the child. Parents do all that they can to instruct their children in a formal way, to teach them what is important, to guide them in the ways of balanced and mature living. The success of their instruction, however, depends upon how much of what they are teaching is really a part of themselves. If there is mutual and genuine love in their home, if as parents they live rigidly by the principles of absolute honesty and fair play, if they manifest understanding, respect, and unselfishness toward each other, if their motivations are spiritual rather than materialistic, then these

[2] "Home Control" (editorial), *The Lutheran Witness,* LXXVI (Dec. 3, 1957), 11.

circumstances become a part of the child's environment and are absorbed by it as the natural way of living. Parents' actions are therefore much more important than their words. Sometimes what they are and do speaks so loudly that their children cannot hear a word that they say.

Parents Share What They Have

Parents cannot pass on to their children that which they do not first of all have. Even in nature we do not expect a stream to rise above its source. Unless parents set for their children the example of what they want them to become, they have no reason to expect their children to be more than they themselves are. Parents cannot expect in their children any more virtues than they themselves instill in them. They can hardly expect to find loyalty and honesty and prayerfulness and conscientiousness in their children if they do not have it themselves. Children are quick to spot hypocrisy. They must see in their parents what they should become. No wonder a child feels conflict when after years of instruction about kindness and fair play he hears his mother "take apart" a social acquaintance over a cup of tea. What shall the child think of all his parents' attempts to instill in him a love for the church when he hears his parents criticize the pastor mercilessly or brutally condemn the action of a congregational committee? What will be the concept of honesty that he has if his father talks to him about honesty, but then refuses to pay a legitimate bill or looks for ways in which he can hedge on his income tax?

Parents must at least have goals if they want to communicate these goals to their children and to the future generation. This makes satisfactory adjustments in the relationship of the parents to each other so very important. They themselves must be growing into a unity before they can receive children into their unity and display to their children what such unity means.

RESPONSIBILITY TO CHILDREN

The responsibilities of parents are great. They have brought their children into the world, and now both God and man hold them responsible for seeing to it that they are nurtured and reared, that their religious training is developed, and that their personal needs, emotional, material, educational, medical, are adequately taken care of. They are expected to be parents in fact as well as in name to *each* of their children, devoting to each a great amount of time and attention in order that they might be equipped with that which only parents can give them for life. Conscious attention must be paid them to help them grow into the unity of the family circle.

As responsibilities of parenthood, these are always responsibilities of love. Parents never perform any of these functions merely out of feelings of obligation, but because it is the only way that a responsible Christian parent knows how to act. In the process there will be many sacrifices in time and energy, in money and pleasure, and even in material advantage. But it never looks or feels like a sacrifice to the parent. He considers it rather a privilege because of the love he has for his family. No amount of wealth could ever begin to compensate for the riches he knows in the love of his family circle. Parenthood to him is the highest privilege a man could know on earth, because it provides opportunity for the parents together to extend themselves and to give a part of the happiness they share, yes, a vital part of themselves, to their growing family circle.

Parenthood is a great deal more than merely a biological process. It is a marvelous blessing. It is at the same time a sacred trust. It is not to be entered into lightly or haphazardly. Certainly it ought to be entered into prayerfully. Parents must be aware of all the responsibilities and obligations that they assume in having a family. God and society, and certainly the children themselves, have a right to expect that children be supplied with adequate provision for a healthy life physically, emotionally, and spiritually. There is a Fourth Commandment which instructs children to honor their father and their mother, and there is also a commandment which instructs father and mother to do everything within their means for their children to earn that honor and respect.

Think, for example, of some Bible passages such as these:

"You shall love the Lord, your God, with all your heart and with all your soul, and with all your might. And these words which I command you this day shall be upon your heart; and you shall teach them diligently to your children, and shall talk of them when you sit in your house, and when you walk by the way, and when you lie down, and when you rise." (Deuteronomy 6:7 RSV)

"Train up a child in the way he should go, and when he is old, he will not depart from it." (Proverbs 22:6 RSV)

"Children ought not to lay up for their parents, but parents for their children." (2 Corinthians 12:14 RSV)

"Fathers, do not provoke your children to anger, but bring them up in the discipline and instruction of the Lord." (Ephesians 6:4 RSV. See also Colossians 3:21)

"He must manage his own household well, keeping his children submissive and respectful in every way." (1 Timothy 3:4 RSV)

Parents owe their children the best that they can give them, spiritually first of all, of course, but also materially.

THE SIZE OF THE FAMILY

The number of children one is able to rear, taking into consideration one's health, financial status, emotional stability, and ability to provide for them adequately according to set standards of our society (as far as higher education, good books, good music, time to do things with the children, etc., are concerned) will vary from family to family. Certainly as it is within the area of Christian stewardship to plan and budget our finances, to plan and budget our time, to plan and budget our energies, it is also within the area of Christian stewardship to plan for our families and to use our best consecrated Christian common sense in making arrangements to provide adequately for them.

Not to want children or to postpone the coming of children unduly is certainly in conflict with the concept that children are a blessing of God. No Christian could ever think of rejecting a blessing of God. Many current attitudes toward the limitation of family size are due to the materialistic influences of our civilization. People sometimes think of children as an economic liability, and they feel much more comfortable with their money invested in securities than in children, who for their entire life will represent a financial outlay. Others feel they cannot assume the responsibility of parenthood until they see themselves comfortably situated with all the conveniences that are normally considered a part of gracious living. The industrialization of our age has also brought about the phenomenon of working wives, and many ladies mistakenly view a career in the business or professional world as more useful than that of homemaker and mother.

They also prefer the additional luxury that money will buy and sometimes even rationalize themselves into believing that they are "sacrificing" the privilege of having a family for the service they can render in a profession. Any self-centered or selfish reason for not having children, or a limited number of them, is never right or God-pleasing. Selfishness is always wrong.

On the other hand, careful, consecrated, thoughtful planning done out of love and consideration for those who are being brought into the world and for those who are bringing them into the world is always in order. It is, in fact, a Christian necessity. Whether there be two or twelve children in a family, each child is entitled to all of the security, affection, love, and attention that the parents are able to give it. Children are a heritage of the Lord. And in this process the parents are still husband and wife to each other — and continue to spend time in their growing unity. They must have time for this in order that they might have something to pass on to the children they are giving to the next generation.

CHAPTER TEN

The Complexity of the Family Unit

The family is a complex organization. It is composed of individuals, each of whom has needs and drives and desires, each of whom is striving for recognition and self-expression and who must make adjustments in his relationship with the others in his family circle. How complex a unit the family is often escapes us until we begin to analyze its structure and its component parts. Understanding something about the challenges involved in family living better prepares us to approach the situation with intelligence and insight.

Complexity of Interpersonal Relationships

When a man and a woman become married, there are but two people to adjust to each other. There is but one interpersonal relationship to satisfy, that between husband and wife. This in itself is no simple task. As we have been indicating throughout this book, it demands a lifetime of intelligent, mature effort on the part of two people to understand and to adjust fully to each other. But now as additional lives are brought into the household, the situation becomes more complicated. When a child is born into the union, there is no longer one, but three interpersonal relationships to adjust to — that between husband and wife (and all previously established routines and patterns and adjustments that they have made need to be re-examined, because the advent of the newcomer changes also the relationship that they have with each other), that between father and child, and that between mother and child. Not only are there now three different sets of interpersonal relationships, but in the closeness of family life each relationship affects also the others. When the family has two children, the number of interpersonal relationships jumps to six — the relationship of the father and mother to each other, the relationship of father to child number one, the relationship of father to child number two, the relationship of mother to child number one, the relationship of mother to child number two, and the relationship of child number one to child number two. Each of these relationships is extremely important and must be nurtured with tender care. If one is neglected in favor of another, the emotions and reactions of individual human beings will be affected, and problems of one sort or another will arise. If the family has three children, the number of interpersonal relationships is already ten. With four children there are fifteen, with five there are twenty-one, and with six children there are twenty-eight. A mathematical formula has been devised to determine the number of interpersonal relationships in any household. If y is the number of persons living in the family unit and x is the number of interpersonal relationships that exist in that household, then $x = \dfrac{(y^2 - y)}{2}$.

When a child is born into the family, new interpersonal relationships are established, each of which must be met satisfactorily. But more than that. With the arrival of each newcomer the previously established relationships change too. It is never simply a matter of everyone's making a few adjustments here and there to make room for the newcomer. The newcomer creates for the family a situation entirely different from what it had before. It may be a pleasant one, but it is nevertheless a different one and a more complicated one. The new arrival may affect the relationship of the other children to each other, or the attitudes of the other children to their parents, or the attitudes of the parents toward the other children. The youngest child is no longer the youngest child and must find a new role. The oldest child may have to assume more responsibility than it had before. The middle child needs help in understanding whether he is "too young to play with his older brother" or "too old to play with his baby brother," and to discover where he fits. The presence of the newcomer affects also the pattern of family living, the routines, the manner in which time and money are shared, the attention that is given to each. The arrival of the new member of the family makes the family entirely different from what it was before, and imposes a completely new set of problems that must be met.

Have you ever noticed how the family routine seems to become less complicated when one or the other member is away for a time? It is not just that there is one less person's schedule to adjust to. The entire family structure is less complicated. If, for example, there are four children in your family, there are fifteen interpersonal relationships involved in your family living. $(x = \frac{(y^2 - y)}{2}; x = \frac{36 - 6}{2} = 15)$. Now if father is away on a business trip for a few days, there are only five persons in the home and only ten, *five fewer,* interpersonal relationships, $\frac{(25 - 5)}{2}$. If, on the other hand, additional people visit the home, the structure becomes more complicated. When grandparents, for example, come to visit, it means more than merely two more plates to place on the table and another bed to make. Our family of six with *fifteen* interpersonal relationships now suddenly finds itself with *twenty-eight* interpersonal relationships.

Grandparents know what this means. They love to have their grandchildren pay them a visit, but they are often exhausted when they leave. No wonder! Grandparents have become accustomed to living with but *one* interpersonal adjustment to make. Now when a family of five moves in for a few days, they suddenly find themselves with *twenty-one* interpersonal relationships. They are not accustomed to such a complicated structure, and physically they are not capable of the rapid adjustment. The natural result is "nervousness."

INTERACTING INFLUENCES OF THE FAMILY

The family is literally an "arena of interacting activities." The experience of one member of the family affects also every other member. Mother, for example, is ill, and not only is the entire family pattern and routine upset, but so is the relationship of each member to the other. The fourth child has the measles, and every member of the family must make adjustments, both physically and psychologically. The second child starts out for his first day of school, and every member of the family takes note of that important occasion. Father is in a gloomy mood, and every single interpersonal relationship is affected because of it. Dad has just closed a big business deal, the much-needed rain came at just the right time, the last pay check showed a substantial raise, and everyone in the family experiences an atmosphere of optimism that interacts. Jane has fallen in love, Jack has learned how to drive, Grandmother has come for a visit, Dick's team has won the important ball game, Mary got the coveted role in the school play, Mother bought a new hat — and each of these activities has an interacting effect upon each of the other members of the family. Whatever influences one member of a family has an influence upon all. Thus also life outside the family, as it affects anyone in the family, will affect the family's relationship with one another.

CHANGING PATTERN OF INDIVIDUALS IN THE FAMILY

This is still not all that is to be said about the family. Individuals within a family structure are changing continually. They are in a constant state of development. Begin with the little child. Each stage of his growth means developmental tasks for him to accomplish. In the stage of infancy and early childhood he must learn how to take solid foods, how to walk, and how to control body elimination. He has the task of achieving physiological stability, of forming simple concepts of social and physical reality, of learning to relate himself emotionally to his parents, siblings, and other people, and of learning how to distinguish between right and wrong. For him each accomplishment is a major feat.

Moving into the middle childhood period, he must learn the physical skills necessary for ordinary purposes. He must build wholesome attitudes toward himself as a growing organism; he must learn to get along with agemates; he must learn an appropriate sex role; he must develop fundamental skills in reading, writing, and calculating, proper attitudes toward social groups and institutions, and certainly as a Christian, a living association with Christ.

In the adolescent stage he has new roles to take and developmental tasks to attain. He now has to accept a masculine or feminine role, adjust to new relationships with agemates of both sexes, become emotionally independent of both parents and other adults, achieve something of an assurance of economic independence, select and begin to prepare for an occupation, develop intellectual skills and concepts necessary for civic competition, achieve socially responsible behavior, apply the Christian principles that he has learned to his expanding world, and prepare himself for marriage and family life.

Next he moves into early adulthood, and again he must grow. He has these tasks to move into: he must select a mate, learn to live with his marriage partner, start a family, rear children, manage a home, get started in an occupation, take on civic and church responsibilities, and find a congenial social group satisfactory to all family members.

This development and adjustment continues all his life. As he moves into middle age, he must play an adult leadership role in civic and social responsibilities, establish and maintain an economic standard of living, assist his teen-age children to become happy and responsible adults, develop some adult leisure-time activities, accept and adjust to the physiological changes of middle age, and adjust to the problems presented by his own aging parents.

Finally he himself comes into the period of later maturity. Again his adjustments are manifold. He must adjust to decreasing physical strength, stamina, and health, to retirement and reduced income, and possibly to the death of his spouse. He must establish an explicit affiliation with his age group and arrange for satisfactory physical living arrangements.[1]

Life is a matter of constant growth and development. No individual is the same from one day to the next. The events of one day change him to make him different the next day.

Changing Patterns in the Family

As individuals grow and develop and change, the family unit does too. As the individual has a personality as an individual, the family has a "personality" as a family. No

[1] The preceding six paragraphs are adapted from Robert Havighurst, *Developmental Tasks and Education* (Chicago, Ill.: University of Chicago Press, 1945).

family is ever the same for any two successive days. As the individuals have changed from day to day, so the composite picture that those individuals compose, the family, too, is a different family from day to day. No two children are ever born into the same family any more than two people step into the same stream of water ten minutes apart. The popular notion that children of the same family have the same environment is not true. Each is part of the same unit, but each is a different part of the unit, and each comes into a unit that is different. In a sense they do not even have the same parents. With each successive child the parents become more experienced; they have had to intertwine themselves in a more complicated mesh of interpersonal relationships. They have become older and more mature. With the experiences of rearing one child they have become a different set of parents for the rearing of another. Child number two and child number three are born into a family structure completely different from that of child number one, and the parents in turn will be different people by the time child number three arrives.

In his widely read column Sydney Harris comments about this in an article entitled "Parents Change, Not the Babies." He says in part:

"It's the third baby that's so wonderful," said the young mother to me at dinner. "I don't know why, but the third one is alway the quietest and easiest to handle."

She had asked me about my new son, and I told her he was a dream. She then said that her children got "better" as they came along.

What she meant, of course, is that she got "better." She was less anxious, less nervous, less worried, less strange with a strange little creature.

We speak about a "first child." But, strictly speaking, there are no first children — there are only first parents. Each child comes into the world only once, and alone; it knows nothing of parents or brothers and sisters. All begin at the same starting line.

It is the parents who change, who become better, more relaxed, more familiar with the taxing and often tedious routine of tending an infant. The third child is usually "good" because he does not feel the hot breath of parental anxiety blowing on the back of his head.[2]

A family's status is never static. It also changes. It also has developmental tasks to achieve.

There is the early stage of marriage. The couple is busy making many adjustments — economic, sexual, in the areas of authority and accountability, in establishing working relationships on a par basis with kin and peers, church and community, and in their social and occupational life.

In the pregnant stage of marriage the expectant parents are making ready for a new constellation of emotional attachments, and once again all the patterns of authority and accountability, of getting and spending income, and many other adjustments need to be revised. How well this second stage of marital adjustment is met depends to a large extent upon how successful and satisfactory the adjustments were in the first stage. Life together is a building process in which one stone is laid upon another. Poor adjustments in one stage make it impossible to make good adjustments in succeeding ones.

Soon children come. Again there are adjustments to the children and to each other. The family continues to develop together, and before long it is a school-age family. New demands, attitudes, and interests play into the picture. Again, how well the family meets the situation in a way satisfactory

[2] Sydney Harris, "Parents Change, Not the Babies," in "Strictly Personal," a syndicated column, Des Moines *Register,* Dec. 23, 1960, p. 6.

to all depends upon how well it has matured in the area of interpersonal relationships in its earlier stages and how well it has grown together into a family unit.

In order not to lose our bearings we must remember that the child is the product of his home environment. He is going through the various stages of family development together with the rest of his family. He is a part of the unit. If there are maladjustments in his family life, the impact will influence him. He will not be as certain of his own stature and role in the situation and will be less secure. His maturity, attitudes, sense of belonging, self-confidence and initiative, his ability to adjust to others will be influenced by what his home life has been and is. Perhaps even his physical condition will be affected by it.

COMPLEXITY OF FAMILY ADJUSTMENTS

Thinking about all the elements that go into making adjustments and living together in a happy home makes one realize what a tremendous task it is and what it means to say that "happy marriages don't just happen; they are made" — made with constant, self-sacrificing, prayerful, and co-operative effort on the part of everyone involved. And tempering every attitude must be a generous sprinkling of Christian love, which begets patience and understanding and thoughtfulness of others. It is the capacity to give and to receive love that makes possible the launching of successful and happy home lives.

Now when in addition the individuals in the home are Christians, also their love is affected by their regeneration. They are "new creatures" when they have been remade by Christ. Their love is built upon the pattern of the love of Christ for them. It is always "other-directed." More and more "self-directedness" recedes. More and more the Christian understands that self-love is really not love at all. It is a negation of love. Love, genuine Christian love, must always be concerned with other people. It is this love that makes the home, that binds it together, and that enables people to live together in harmony and satisfaction.

Realizing not only the internal complications of family living, but also the fact that many aspects of our culture have an influence upon the family, every Christian church body is putting forth efforts to assist people in understanding the dynamics of family living and in helping them to establish goals and aims, and to achieve them. For the Christian Family Week observance of The Lutheran Church — Missouri Synod in 1951 a tract was produced that has enjoyed wide distribution. It was the result of a workshop of forty-nine churchmen who undertook drawing up a Christian Family Charter. The charter that they produced is the following:

A STANDARD FOR THE CHRISTIAN FAMILY

God Made Us a Family

We Need One Another
We Love One Another
We Forgive One Another

We Work Together
We Play Together
We Worship Together

Together We Use God's Word
Together We Grow in Christ
Together We Love All Men
Together We Serve Our God
Together We Hope for Heaven

These Are Our Hopes and Ideals
Help Us to Attain Them, O God
Through Jesus Christ, Our Lord [3]

In the light of the many complications of family living, every Christian family ought to read together and discuss this standard again and again and to rededicate themselves to its principles.

CHAPTER ELEVEN

Family Growth

The preceding chapter touched briefly upon some of the adjustments that families must make as families as they progress from one stage of their development to another. Each of these stages of family development contains some aspects to which some special attention should be given. Husbands and wives should be aware of some of these factors in order to move intelligently in the direction of family unity and harmony. If family unity must be *developed,* then the more we understand the dynamics of family living, and the more we understand what happens to families, the more intelligently we will be able to build.

For our purposes we shall divide the family development into six stages:

1. Early Marriage

[3] This Standard is interpreted in Oscar Feucht's *Helping Families Through the Church* (St. Louis: Concordia Publishing House, 1971), pp. 24—27.

2. The Pregnant Stage

3. The Preschool-Children Stage

4. The School-Age Stage

5. Middle Age

6. Old Age

1. EARLY MARRIAGE

a. THE HONEYMOON

This is the first opportunity that young couples have of really getting to know each other as husband and wife. Its purpose is not primarily to embark upon some activity which either or both of them have always wanted to do, nor is it merely to get away, perhaps even together with other people. The honeymoon is for the couple to spend the first days and weeks of their marriage together in a setting where each might begin to get accustomed to his new role, to share the other's interests, and to make initial adjustments to each other. The purpose of the honeymoon is best fulfilled if the couple is able to get away to a place of rest and quiet *alone*, where they can in a relaxed atmosphere devote themselves to learning to know each other. The distant and glamorous places may not serve the purpose as well as one very near by. Normally long trips and excursions are tiring and wearing on nerves, thus making it difficult for people to give themselves to each other as fully as they ought, and defeating the chief purpose of the honeymoon.

In this period the initial sexual adjustments are made. It is very normal that at this time both husband and wife will be expecting to show their loves to each other. The initial experience of the newly given freedom and intimacy is something to which neither is accustomed and which may make both of them somewhat uncomfortable. It is, however, a trip into a gloriously wonderful adventure of love. This period, free from the responsibilities and cares of the workaday world, and one in which the new husband and wife have no other pressures on their mind but to give their total selves to each other, is the ideal way and time for the young people to get to "know" each other.

Both need to remember, however, that they are merely in the beginning stages of the physical aspect of their marriage. Their relations together might be truly delightful and mutually satisfying from the very beginning. On the other hand, the initial sexual experiences might not be as mutually pleasurable as they had envisioned. Most often they are not. The art of love-making grows with experience. The physical adjustments of marriage, just like every other adjustment, develop with practice. The honeymoon is the opportunity for either or both of the newly married people to hurdle any initial fears and qualms concerning the sexual relationship. It provides the setting for the beginning of their adventure into this new realm. The honeymoon is not the ultimate peak of perfection in marriage; it is only the beginning. The building of a marriage might be likened to the construction of a great cathedral. It takes a lifetime. There may be trouble fitting all the blocks together, but under God's blessing, with time and effort and Christian dedication, steady strides will be made in the building process.

b. FAMILY DEVOTIONS

Already on the first day of their married life, husbands and wives should begin to establish a pattern of family devotions together. This might seem like the natural thing for a Christian couple to do, particularly if they come from homes where this is the pattern. Such, however, is not always the case. The Christian husband should take the lead in establishing this pattern for his home. If he comes from a home where this was not the practice, he may feel at a loss at how to begin. If family devotions were the practice in his own home, he still will have some difficulties. The likelihood is that someone else was the responsible head of his home and thus took the leadership role in this regard. The husband must now assume a new role in this area, a role in which he feels strange. He now becomes, as the head of his home, responsible for its spiritual atmosphere. In all likelihood he will feel somewhat awkward in this role at first, but it is one custom whose establishment should not be postponed until "later," or "until we get established in our home." Christian husbands and wives have much to thank God for in bringing them together into the married estate; they have great need of God's blessings upon this new venture of theirs; they have many things to lay before the throne of God's grace together; they have many spiritual insights and Christian virtues to develop for their life together.

Every couple should discuss with its pastor, before the wedding itself (certainly later if it has not been done before), the availability of relevant helps and the different patterns that their devotions might take. The spiritual returns of family devotions will be rich and rewarding.

C. THE MENSTRUAL PERIOD

Even though a husband has lived in a home where his mother has undergone the regular menstrual cycle, and even though he may have had sisters in his family, he still is not aware from them of what really happens. He must learn early in his marriage that many women often experience emotional conflicts and tensions in connection with their menstrual period. The reproductive system is closely tied to the nervous system. It is at this time that she may become moody, perhaps sarcastic, and often depressed. Her outlook toward life may become rather pessimistic. She becomes more than ordinarily sensitive, may display bursts of temper and crying spells. Criticism affects her much more deeply than usual. This is one of the times when arguments and differences can readily arise. Husbands must be aware of this situation and be especially lavishing with their tenderness, patience, and kindness. The moods of some women are affected several days before the menstruation actually begins. These are difficult times also for the husband, because he cannot understand fully what is happening and is not always aware that his wife's "period" has begun or is about to begin. All the understanding and love and avoidance of critical decisions or situations that he can effect in this period will be more than amply rewarded by her appreciation later.

Many times women think of menstruation as the "woman's burden" or "the monthly curse." They think of its discomfort, its inconvenience, its hygienic factors. Menstruation is not a curse; it is a blessing. It is a reminder every month of the high and holy privilege that God has given to womanhood. He has designed her body so that she can be a partaker with God in the most wonderful miracle on earth. It is a reminder to her that God has constituted her body so that she can share in the blessedness of motherhood. Concentrating on the spiritual implications of menstruation rather than on the physical aspects will help to make the period not only endurable, but even beautiful, for the Christian woman.

d. AFTER TWO OR THREE YEARS

After a period of time the strong romantic aspect of love that helps tie husband and wife together in the early years of marriage begins to fade. Their hearts no longer skip a beat when the other approaches. They no longer feel the same ecstasy of delight and thrill simply from being touched by the other. That strange sense of well-being and buoyancy that they feel in each other's presence may no longer be so strong. They begin to see that the individual they married is quite human after all. They must make adjustments to all of the weaknesses that they see in each other. His "angel" is after all quite human, and her "dream boy" is down-to-earth flesh and blood. They find themselves having differences of opinion. Each seems to have changed since courtship days.

When this happens, many couples feel that they are "falling out of love," that the other "doesn't love them any more," and what is sometimes worse, that their marriage is not a happy one, and that perhaps it was a mistake. Couples need to be aware of what is happening to them at this time. They are not necessarily losing their love for each other. In the true Christian marriage, love is beginning to mature into the deeper, more steady love that results in a more profound, more closely knit oneness. Romantic love is a wonderful gift of God to help young people over their first major adjustments together, but it is a love upon which the deeper, steady love of marriage is built. Once they understand that, couples are ready to build their lives together solidly and realistically toward a beautiful unity.

2. THE PREGNANCY STAGE

When a woman becomes pregnant, this ought to be a time of real joy for both husband and wife. The first pregnancy is, however, a new experience for the woman. Her emotions will very likely be mingled with both joy and fear. There are apt to be many strange contradictions in her attitudes. At times she will think of the personal sacrifices that she will have to make, the way her life will be altered, the extra chores, and all this, together with the physical discomfort of pregnancy and the self-consciousness about her shape, may at times cause her to give expression to contradictory feelings. She might even verbalize the thought that she wishes she were not pregnant. Husbands must not at this time assume that she does not want the child or will not love it. They must not forget that she may evidence extremes of emotional behavior at this time, either extreme well-being or moments of depression. In any event a nine-month period is a long time. The anticipation of any event for a nine-month period is a nervous strain for any human being. These are days that call for an added amount of understanding and concern for her.

When the first child is born, something happens to the parents that only they who have experienced it can understand. The father suddenly feels more like an adult. The wonderful feeling of a completely dependent new life, one for whom he is responsible, creates in him a maturity of outlook that is difficult to describe. His responsibilities toward home and toward church, the awareness of having to set an example, the importance of the things that really count suddenly burst upon him. With mothers much the same thing happens. The radiance and joy that she feels gives her a glow that gives expression to all the inward beauty of her soul. It is as she cares for her child that one sees her real, tender, loving, sacrificing self fully blossom.

There is no room in the glories of parenthood for self-pity. If the husband displays attitudes of resentment because his wife's attention to the new baby prevents her from doing as much for him as she did before the child was born, he is manifesting immaturities which as an adult in marriage he should work to overcome. Any mother who resents the sacrifices she is called upon to make in the giving of herself to her new baby has not learned the meaning of real love. This is an event in which both together should rejoice. It presents a challenge that should be an exciting experience for both of them as they work together in the rearing of their child. They see God's finger in this event. They understand that "children are a heritage of the Lord, and the fruit of the womb is His reward." (Psalm 127:3)

3. Preschool Children

This is perhaps one of the most nerve-racking and hectic times, physically speaking, in married life. It is especially the mother who feels the brunt of this because of her continual association with the growing children in the home. God manifested His wisdom in limiting the time of childbirth to the younger years of adult life, to the time when parents still have the physical energies to take up the demands of child-rearing. Youngsters need to be trained in every aspect of interpersonal living. Their energies are boundless, and their exploratory instincts sometimes exasperating. The care and attention that the children need and demand in a physical way make it impossible sometimes for mother to keep up with all her responsibilities. She is always finding herself behind in the work she wants to accomplish, and often breathes a sigh of relief when finally the little bundles of energy are tucked away into bed. Harried mothers need not only the patience and understanding of their husbands, they also need a helping hand just to keep going.

This is also a time when young parents must expect to make many sacrifices as far as their social life is concerned. Their new responsibilities tie them rather closely to their home. The demands of their children do not allow them to be as free in their involvement and contribution to church and community as they should like to be. The occasional baby sitter helps considerably, and husbands and wives must on occasion free themselves for some time away from their children. This they need to keep a proper perspective. Instead of feeling sorry for themselves during this time, parents should rather concentrate on enjoying every precious moment and every new stage of development in their growing youngsters. It offers them the opportunity to see real love in action, the kind of love that gives and sacrifices cheerfully. Parents who are given this opportunity to develop a real spirit of involvement with their children have advantages that childless homes do not have. The exercise of this kind of love enriches them and provides for them the kind of love that makes their relationship to each other more outgoing too.

4. THE SCHOOL-AGE STAGE

This is a period of increased activity for all members of the family. The children's interests outside the home begin to take up also some of the parents' time. They want to be and ought to be a part of their children's school life and church life. As the children grow and become involved in activities, schedules become complicated with additional meetings and chaperoning and chauffeuring. Instead of having all the children home at the same time, some or all the children may be gone to one function or another. This can be an extremely frustrating period. Mother is unable to keep up with all the interests and schedules, or at least she feels this way, and she longs for the days when the family could express its unity and solidarity by being together.

During this time each member of the family needs to feel a deep personal security. If the relationship of the family is marked by a genuine feeling of love and security and unity, then each member of the family will carry this feeling of well-being with him no matter where he goes or what he does. It is not so much the physical togetherness that develops the bonds of family unity as the *feeling* of togetherness. One's feeling of security comes not so much from the number of hours he is together with his family as from how he feels and reacts toward those hours, and what those hours do to him. It is this feeling of togetherness that every family ought to struggle to achieve. Every member of the family — whether he is at work or at play, whether he is seated around the dinner table or whether he is in the service thousands of miles away, whether he is on a business trip or getting in shape for a basketball game or out on a date — needs to feel behind him the strong support of a loving unified home. He needs to feel that he is wanted and understood and that what he is doing is being appreciated. It is this assurance that gives one a sense of togetherness.

5. MIDDLE AGE

A critical period for most families is the middle-age period. The hustle and bustle of life with the children in the home is past. The children have moved on to college, are working elsewhere, or are married. The hubbub of family activity ceases, and that at times rather abruptly. Suddenly the family is face to face with a new situation. Its interests no longer revolve completely around the interests of one another. The children no longer are as dependent upon their parents as they were in the preceding years. They have become the adults that their parents wanted them to become. At this time there is a tremendous psychological adjustment that must be made, particularly by the mothers, whose entire lives were wrapped around the welfare of their children. Now suddenly they do not feel as needed and as necessary as they did during the earlier years. They have much more time on their hands, and unless this time is wisely invested in new interests and activities, they might easily become moody and depressed. A new constellation of interests must be developed at this time in order to keep life full and vibrant and to maintain the feeling of usefulness and helpfulness.

It is also during this period that the couple will undergo the involutional period. Everybody, men and women alike, experiences this period with varying symptoms, women generally between the ages of 40 to 55 and men between the age of 60 to 65.

Many pass the period with little or no emotional stress; others experience more difficulty. Among the symptoms that might show themselves are depression in the person who has not previously been subject to it, worry, insomnia, guilt feelings, anxiety, agitation, delusion, preoccupation with physical symptoms (hypochondria), now and then feelings of persecution and suspicion of loved ones. Certainly not all of these symptoms will occur, perhaps not any of them. And if some of them do occur, they may be mild. Psychologists say that the symptoms of the involutional period are most likely to be more severe in persons with a compulsive personality (perfectionists).

Much can be done medically to alleviate the symptoms if

they occur, and doctors' help should be solicited. But not only the patient needs help and guidance and counsel. The other members of the family do too. They may theoretically be aware of what is happening, and yet as they live in the day-by-day situation, they need help to see them through the period, as difficult for them as for the afflicted persons. This period of married life calls for an additional amount of patience, understanding, and prayer. One factor that all loved ones must fix firmly in their minds is that the person manifesting involutional symptoms is not responsible for his emotions or for the way he thinks at this particular time. It is a passing phase of life.

6. OLD AGE

The golden years of life can be ones of extremes in several directions. They can be years filled with satisfaction, service, peace, and contentment, or they can be years filled with loneliness, bitterness, frustration, worry, and fear. Much depends upon two factors: how well couples have planned to meet the circumstances of their later years, and the spiritual resources they have upon which to draw for a peace-filled life.

Preparation for retirement and old age must take place long before retirement time comes. Every couple must do some long-range financial planning and must give some intelligent, objective thought to the physical aspects of their last years together. They must be prepared graciously to accept and make adjustments to the fact that they will have to slow down and that their health will in all likelihood be fading. It is true with most people, no matter what their age, that psychologically they feel no different from what they did when they were younger. The difference is physical. The middle-aged person in spirit feels no older than the adolescent, and the elderly person is not conscious of feeling different in spirit from what he did in middle age. Physically though he is not the same. When one has done some long-range planning for finances, for health, for hobbies, for housing, and has prepared himself early to accept a change of pace, he can be ready at retirement for an exciting era of his life.

Someone has said, "Old people should not be retired, but retreaded for a new phase of life and service." This retreading job is something that the couple can do beautifully together. Where a unity has developed in the home through the years, older people understand that they need each other more in their twilight years than ever before. Whereas in their so-called productive years they concentrated in joining in their influence upon others, their children, their work, they now realize their dependence upon each other. This provides them a rich opportunity to manifest their genuine Christian love in concern for each other. To feel together at this stage of life, to be concerned with the other's welfare as perhaps they have never been before, can bring to each of them the deepest kind of satisfaction, and can help them in discussing and planning and working together in a new kind of life.

Furthermore, both have had a full life that ought to be rich with memories. Reliving these days, recounting the many blessings of God, tracing the finger of God through the pattern of their married life together, is an experience that is denied everyone except those who are older.

Marie Dressler once said, "The real question is not how old you are, but how you are old." [1] Chronological age has nothing to do with one's outlook. Some people are old at forty; others are young at eighty. Developing and keeping

[1] Adams, p. 145.

a healthy, positive, cheerful, Christian outlook toward life makes the difference between a bitter, selfish old man and a cheerful, helpful one.

With increasing longevity, with lower retirement ages and increased economic provisions for the retired, more and more attention is being paid to the senior citizens, who are becoming an increasing proportion of our population. Churches and communities are providing opportunities for fellowship and outlets for service. Some areas are developing housing units with small, economical apartments for the retired. This attention is as it should be. But in the final analysis the quality of their life in age will depend to a great extent upon the inner resources that the couple has developed in their life together. Their deepest joys and satisfactions come, not from what others provide and make possible for them, but from what they can do together. The best preparation for old age therefore is careful attention to the development of their marital unity during their entire life together, beginning the moment that they give themselves to each other at the altar. Every event that happens to them, every experience that they share, every problem that they solve helps determine how they will make future adjustments together, also in old age. Hence the best preparation for a happy life together in the golden years of life is the development of a happy home life in the earlier years of marriage.

A Christian couple will be able to look back upon a life together, replete with blessings from on high, and join David in proclaiming gratefully and humbly: "My mouth will tell of Thy righteous acts, of Thy deeds of salvation all the day, for their number is past my knowledge. With the mighty deeds of the Lord God I will come, I will praise Thy righteousness, Thine alone. O God, from my youth Thou hast taught me, and I still proclaim Thy wondrous deeds. So even to old age and gray hairs, O God, do not forsake me, till I proclaim Thy might to all the generations to come. Thy power and Thy righteousness, O God, reach the high heavens. Thou who hast done great things, O God, who is like Thee?" (Psalm 71:15-19 RSV)

A couple that can express sentiments like these in the latter years of their life together have had a beautiful unity in their marriage.

Appendixes

The following excerpt is from the book *With This Ring* by Louis Burke, Judge of the Superior Court in Los Angeles County, California. This quotation is the section on "Children" included in the Reconciliation Agreement that he devised for husbands and wives having marital difficulties.

CHILDREN

Children bring life to a marriage. There are no dull moments in parenthood. With children a "house" becomes a "home"; the "married couple" becomes a "family." Each parent takes on a new dignity and new responsibility. Teamwork between the parents becomes a necessity.

The coming of children must not be permitted to disturb the warm relationship between husband and wife. One must not neglect the other.

When parents hold their newly-born for the first time, they must ask themselves — Is it possible that we, alone, are responsible for this perfect little bundle of humanity? The answer is obvious to most. They see in the child the handwork of God.

God entrusts to the parents a new life, a body, and a soul. The child is His child and theirs. They become God's agents in the upbringing of the child. And what an awesome responsibility it is! It is estimated that 80 per cent of what a child is, or turns out to be, is attributable directly to his parents, or to those in whom his upbringing is entrusted.

We realize that a child is the outgrowth of the love of its parents, and just as his conception required their joint act, so will each step in his training and development require the love, attention, and self-sacrifice of each parent. We agree that neither of us can do the job alone.

ESSENTIALS FOR NORMAL CHILDHOOD

We agree that if a child is to attain full stature, physically, mentally, and spiritually, he will need many things, including:

1. The love and active interest of each parent.
2. A home, however humble, where harmony prevails.
3. The good example and leadership of his parents in his moral and spiritual development.

4. The assurance that he and each other child in the home is treated fairly and impartially and that no one is loved more than any other.

PARENTS' CONDUCT TOWARD CHILD

We agree that each child has his own individuality and that his training must be planned with his particular needs and abilities definitely in mind.

We agree that our conduct toward our child, or children, shall include the following:

1. We will think and speak of our child as "our" child, never as "my" child or "your" child. The responsibility is joint and will always be that way.

2. We will maintain a united front on matters of policy and discipline. We won't interfere with each other in the administering of discipline. We will settle any differences of opinion out of the presence of the child.

3. We will try to reduce the number of commands or orders which we issue to our child. (A flood of orders turns to "nagging" and becomes meaningless. Their number can be reduced by establishing regular rules and sticking with them and by making use of suggestions, requests, hints, praise, etc. Orders should be based on reason, and most children will profit by a simple statement of the reason. Modest praise for obedience usually helps.)

4. We will try to get the child's full attention before giving an order. His mind may be miles away. We will strive to give orders calmly, in a tone which indicates we expect them to be carried out.

5. We agree never to administer physical punishment while in anger.

6. We will always administer punishment in privacy; we will try not to humiliate the child in front of "the fellas."

7. We will try to answer our child's questions; encourage him to grow up with a wholesome respect for himself, his body, and for others.

8. We will teach him the proper care of his own property and to respect the property of others.

9. We will develop his sense of responsibility by assigning him responsibilities suitable to his age and development.

10. We will help him to develop sound judgment in the choice

of companions. We won't do all the judging for him or impose our own prejudices on him. We realize that someday he will have to rely on his own judgment — that ours won't be available.

11. We will not quarrel in the presence of the child.

12. We will not speak ill of each other in his presence; if it happens inadvertently — we will explain later that we did not mean it.

13. We promise not to unload on him the worries and troubles of adults — he will be a child only once.

SOUND FAMILY RELATIONSHIP

Finally — we will strive to remember that the best discipline is a *loved* and *loving* parent's disapproval of whatever wrongful act the child has done. We know that obedience through fear is short-lived — the child will outgrow the fear, and long before that he will have lost respect. We acknowledge that obedience through love endures and that just as love between husband and wife must be mutual to be effective, so the love of parent and child must be reciprocal — must be earned by both. We have stressed that the disapproval should be of the wrongful act and not of the child, because the distinction is important. It is not the child that is bad, but rather *what he has done* that is inappropriate in the eyes of the parent.

We will strive for patience, gentleness, understanding, firmness, ingenuity, and love in dealing with our child or children. We recognize that these are some of the principal ingredients for a happy relationship.

APPENDIX II

The following is an interpretation of the Christian Family Standard adopted by the Family Life Committee of The Lutheran Church — Missouri Synod. This interpretation is quoted from Feucht's *Helping Families Through the Church,* pp. 24—27.

THE CHRISTIAN FAMILY STANDARD INTERPRETED

God Made Us a Family

We acknowledge that God ordained marriage for the welfare of man and woman, and as the means for continuing the human family. As husband and wife we chose each other and asked God to bless our marriage, which must be kept sacred and unbroken. We also acknowledge children as precious gifts of God and regard them as a sacred trust. We pledge ourselves to live together as a family in a manner pleasing to our heavenly Father.

We Need One Another

We acknowledge the God-established family as providing the ideal environment in which man and woman and their children can best supply one another's needs and find their fullest development and their highest happiness. We pledge ourselves to live for one another in mutual encouragement and helpfulness.

We Love One Another

We acknowledge mutual love and true devotion one to another as the will of God and as a basic human need. We shall constantly endeavor to foster attitudes and expressions of love between husband and wife, children and parents. In good days and in evil days, in strength and in weakness, the love of Christ shall be our pattern.

We Forgive One Another

We acknowledge the boundless grace of God, who for Christ's sake daily forgives all sins to all believers and gives them the peace of a good conscience. As He forgave us, so we seek pardon from each member of the family whom we have offended, and pledge ourselves to extend complete pardon where we have been wronged.

We Work Together

We acknowledge that God has ordained work as the means of supplying our daily needs and that family ties are strengthened by planning and working together. We pledge ourselves to employ our minds and our hands in useful labor and to co-operate in providing for the physical welfare of our family.

We Play Together

We acknowledge the wise provision of God for companionship and recreation as a means for refreshing body and mind. We pledge ourselves to take time to be with one another, to join in recreational activities, and to plan our leisure in the interest of family happiness and unity.

We Worship Together

We acknowledge the worship of God through Christ as a sacred privilege and responsibility and as the effective means of bringing us closer to God and to one another. We pledge ourselves to gather in Christ's name in the family circle and in the Christian congregation, that God may speak to us and that we may speak to Him.

Together We Use God's Word

We acknowledge the Bible as the divine means of bestowing, increasing, and directing faith, as the necessary food for our souls, and as the certain guide for our lives. We pledge ourselves to read and study the Holy Scriptures together and to apply them to our varied needs and problems.

Together We Grow in Christ

We acknowledge that Christ dwells in the hearts of all true believers and by His Holy Spirit causes them to grow in Christian faith, in spiritual understanding, and in godly living. We pledge ourselves to aid one another in the development of Christian personalities and in the practice of Christian virtues.

Together We Love All Men

We acknowledge that in our attitudes and behavior toward our fellow men we should follow our Lord's example. We pledge ourselves to make our family a wholesome influence in the community so that our friends may be served, our enemies won, the righteous fortified, and unbelievers led to praise our Father in heaven.

Together We Serve Our God

We acknowledge that all that we are and have — our life and our time, our talents and possessions — is a trust from God; that all is to be used for His glory and the good of men — in the home, in the Christian congregation, and wherever opportunity presents itself.

Together We Hope for Heaven

We acknowledge that by faith in Christ heaven is even now our possession. We pledge ourselves to live for God and not to center our affections on the things of this world. We commit ourselves to the guidance of the Holy Spirit and pray that our family may in God's own time be united with the whole family of God in our eternal home.

APPENDIX III

GOALS FOR THE MATURING COUPLE, WHICH ARE PARTICULARLY PERTINENT TO A PROGRESSIVELY SUCCESSFUL RELATIONSHIP

(A list compiled by Professor David M. Fulcomer, Iowa State U.)

In distributing this list, Dr. Fulcomer makes the following comments about these goals:

1. They are non-reachable; that is, no couple can rate consistently 100% or anything close to it in regard to any of these goals.
2. They can be useful and important in defining the direction in which a couple should try to move in order to reach the greatest possible success in their relationship.

The Goals:

1. Complete mutual confidence and respect.
2. The full acceptance of each other's strengths and weaknesses.
3. The ability to communicate fully — to "get through to each other" on all matters pertinent to the relationship.
4. Compatible or complementary basic philosophies and values.
5. The ability to understand and use sex properly.
6. The ability to adjust to discords constructively.
7. Full emotional interdependence: the ability to be emotionally independent of each other, and at the same time to be emotionally dependent upon each other.
8. Satisfaction and interest in each other's roles.
9. The possession of full companionship.
10. Couple ability to adapt to social pressures and environment with greatest benefit to outside responsibilities and couple relationships.
11. The ability to express love and affection.
    (These are not listed in the order of importance.)

APPENDIX IV

The following Scripture passages have been culled from the New Testament as dealing in one way or another with one aspect of family living and responsibility. They might be used by husband and wife to study what the New Testament has to say about the home. They would form an excellent basis for private devotion. They might offer beginning helps, too, when one is looking for thoughts to develop organizational devotions.

NEW TESTAMENT PASSAGES RELEVANT TO MARRIAGE, FAMILY, AND HOME LIFE

Passages dealing with home life

Luke 1:6
Luke 10:38-42
John 2:1-10
John 11
John 12
1 Corinthians 7
Ephesians 5:22-33
Ephesians 6:4
Colossians 3:18-21
1 Timothy 3:8-12
1 Peter 3:1-7

Illustrations from home life

Matthew 7:9-12
Matthew 21:28-32
Matthew 25:1-13
Matthew 11:16-19;
 Luke 7:31-50
Luke 15:11-32

Miracles performed in the home

Matthew 8:14, 15;
 Mark 1:30, 31; Luke 4:38-40
Matthew 9:18-26;
 Mark 5:22-43; Luke 8:49-56
Matthew 15:21-28;
 Mark 7:24-30
Matthew 17:14-21;
 Mark 9:17-29; Luke 9:38-42
Luke 7:11-17
Luke 8:43-50

Luke 13:11-17
John 2
John 9:1-14
John 11:1-45

Relationship in marriage

Matthew 19:3-9; Mark 10:2-12
1 Corinthians 7
Ephesians 5:22-33
Colossians 3:18, 19
1 Peter 3:1-7

Passages regarding children

Matthew 7:11
Matthew 11:16, 17;
 Luke 7:31, 32
Matthew 15:1-6; Mark 7:10-13
Matthew 18:1-6
Matthew 19:13-15; Luke 18:
 15-17; Mark 10:13-16
Matthew 19:19
Matthew 21:28-32
Luke 2:41-51
Luke 2:52
Luke 18:20
Galatians 4:1, 2
Ephesians 6:1-4
Colossians 3:20

Passages referring to morals (sex)

Matthew 5:27, 28
Matthew 15:19

Matthew 14:3, 4; Mark 6:17, 18
Luke 18:20
John 4:17, 18
John 8:3-11
Romans 1:26, 27
Romans 13:9, 13, 14
1 Corinthians 5:1
1 Corinthians 6:9-11
1 Corinthians 6:18-20
Galatians 5:19-21
Ephesians 5:3-5
Ephesians 5:11, 12
Colossians 3:5, 6
1 Thessalonians 4:3-5
1 Timothy 2:9
2 Timothy 2:22
2 Timothy 3:2, 3, 6
James 4:4, 5
1 Peter 1:14
1 Peter 4:3
2 Peter 2:1-14

Passages on remaining unmarried

Matthew 19:11, 12
1 Corinthians 7:7-9

Passages regarding divorce

Matthew 5:31, 32
Matthew 19:9
Luke 16:18
1 Corinthians 7:15

Passages referring to women

Matthew 26:6-13; Mark 14:3-9
Matthew 27:19

Matthew 27:55, 56;
   Luke 23:27-31
Matthew 28:1-10; Mark 16:
   1-11; Luke 24; John 20
Luke 1:1-60
Luke 2:36-38
Luke 3:41-52
Luke 21:1-3
John 4:7-42
John 11
Acts 16:13-19; 18:26
1 Corinthians 7
1 Corinthians 11:3-16
1 Corinthians 14:34, 35
Ephesians 5:22-33
Colossians 3:18, 19
1 Timothy 2:9-15
1 Timothy 5:1-16
2 Timothy 1:5
Titus 2:3-5
1 Peter 3:1-7
2 John

Passages for deeper study

Matthew 8:21, 22
Matthew 10:35; Luke 12:53
Matthew 12:46-50;
   Mark 3:31-35; Luke 8:19-21
Matthew 19:7-9; Mark 10:2-12
Matthew 19:10, 11
Matthew 19:29; Luke 14:26
Matthew 20:21-28
John 2:4 compared with
   John 19:26
1 Corinthians 7:7-9

Bibliography

Belgum, David. *Engagement.* St. Louis: Concordia Publishing House, 1972.

Bowman, Henry A. *Marriage for Moderns.* 5th ed. New York: McGraw-Hill, 1965.

Bracher, Marjory. *Love Is No Luxury.* Philadelphia: Muhlenberg, 1968.

Bueltmann, A. J. *Happiness Is Homemade.* St. Louis: Concordia Publishing House, 1971.

Clinebell, Howard and Charlotte. *The Intimate Marriage.* New York: Harper and Row, 1970.

Cressman, Rhoda G. *So You're Going to Be Parents.* Scottdale, Pa.: Herald Press, 1968.

Denton, Wallace. *Family Problems and What to Do About Them.* Philadelphia: Westminster Press, 1971.

Duvall, Evelyn M. *Love and the Facts of Life.* New York: Association Press, 1963.

———. *Why Wait Until Marriage?* New York: Association Press, 1965.

Fairchild, Roy W. *Christians in Families.* Richmond, Va.: The Covenant Life Curriculum Press, 1964.

Feucht, Oscar, ed. *Helping Families Through the Church: A Symposium on Family Life Education.* St. Louis: Concordia Publishing House, 1971.

———. Paul G. Hansen, Fred Kramer, and Erwin L. Lueker. *Engagement and Marriage: A Sociological, Historical, and Theological Investigation of Engagement and Marriage.* St. Louis: Concordia Publishing House, 1959.

———. Harry G. Coiner, Alfred von Rohr Sauer, and Paul G. Hansen. *Sex and the Church: A Sociological, Historical, and Theological Investigation of Sex Attitudes.* St. Louis: Concordia Publishing House, 1961.

———. *Family Relationships and the Church: A Sociological, Historical, and Theological Study of Family Structures, Roles, and Relationships.* St. Louis: Concordia Publishing House, 1970.

Gesch, Roy. *A Wife Prays.* St. Louis: Concordia Publishing House, 1968.

———. *A Husband Prays.* St. Louis: Concordia Publishing House, 1968.

———. *Parents Pray.* St. Louis: Concordia Publishing House, 1968.

Grams, Armin. *The Christian Encounters Changes in Family Life.* St. Louis: Concordia Publishing House, 1968.

Hansen, Paul. *Newlyweds.* St. Louis: Concordia Publishing House, 1972.

Harnik, Bernard. *Risk and Chance in Marriage.* Waco, Tex.: Word Books, 1972.

Hulme, William. *Firstborn.* St. Louis: Concordia Publishing House, 1972.

Jackson, Edgar N. *When Someone Dies.* Philadelphia: Fortress Press, 1971.

Knight, James A. *For the Love of Money.* Philadelphia: Lippincott Co., 1968.

Landis, Paul H. *Making the Most of Marriage.* New York: Appleton-Century-Crofts, 1969.

Lee, Robert and Casebier, Marjorie. *The Spouse Gap.* Nashville: Abingdon Press, 1971.

Mace, David R. *Getting Ready for Marriage.* Nashville: Abingdon Press, 1972.

Marriage Counseling Cards. St. Louis: Concordia Publishing House, 1972.

Marriage Magazine. St. Meinrad, Ind.: St. Meinrad Archabbey.

May, Edward C. *Family Worship Idea Book.* St. Louis: Concordia Publishing House, 1965.

Parent Education Materials Packet. National Lutheran Parent-Teacher League, 3558 So. Jefferson Ave., St. Louis, Mo. 63118.

Peterson, James A. *Married Love in the Middle Years.* New York: Association Press, 1968.

Pike, James A. *If You Marry Outside Your Faith.* New York: Harper and Brothers, 1954.

Piper, Otto A. *The Christian Interpretation of Sex.* New York: Charles Scribner's Sons, 1951.

Rainier, Jerome and Julia. *Sexual Pleasure in Marriage.* New York: Simon and Schuster, 1969.

Simon, Paul and Jeanne. *Protestant-Catholic Marriages Can Succeed.* New York: Association Press, 1967.

Temple, E. J. *Focus on Marriage.* St. Louis: Concordia Publishing House, 1973.

Toelke, Otto W. *In the Presence of God.* St. Louis: Concordia Publishing House, 1962.

Vayhinger, John. *Before Divorce.* Philadelphia: Fortress Press, 1972.

Wrage, Karl. *Man and Woman: The Basis of Sex and Marriage.* Philadelphia: Fortress Press, 1969.